LIBERTY

EQUALITY

and

FRATERNITY

By

Fulton J. Sheen

Bishop Sheen Today
280 John Street
Midland, Ontario, Canada
L4R 2J5
www.bishopsheentoday.com

Unless otherwise noted, Scripture quotations in the main text are taken from the Douay-Rheims edition of the Old and New Testaments, public domain.

Library of Congress Cataloging-in-Publication Data

Names: Sheen, Fulton J. (Fulton John), 1895-1979, author.

Smith, Allan J, editor.

Sheen, Fulton J. (Fulton John), 1895-1979, Liberty, Equality and Fraternity; by Fulton J. Sheen. Registered in the name of Fulton J. Sheen, under Library of Congress catalog card number: A 123537, following publication November 9, 1938.

Nihil Obstat: Arthur J. Scanlan, S.T.D. Censor librorum

Imprimatur: Stephen J. Donahue, D.D. Adm. New York, September 18, 1938

Title: Liberty, Equality and Fraternity.

Identifiers: ISBN: 978-1-990427-22-0 (paperback)
ISBN: 978-1-990427-23-7 (eBook)

ISBN: 978-1-990427-82-4(hardcover)

Fulton J. Sheen; compiled by Allan J. Smith.

Includes bibliographical references

Subjects: Jesus Christ — Liberty – Equality - Fraternity

DEDICATED TO

MARY IMMACULATE

GATE OF HEAVEN

THROUGH WHICH

MEN PASS AS BROTHERS

EQUAL IN THEIR NATURE

TO THE GLORIOUS LIBERTY

OF THE CHILDREN OF GOD

Introduction

The world today stands in need of two virtues, justice, and charity. These two virtues are the only effective cures for two evils, one the accidental evil of capitalism, the other the essential evil of Communism; capitalism, on the one hand, with its abuse of concentrated wealth and privilege and its subjection of millions to the lot of insecure wage-earners; and Communism, on the other hand, with its class-hatred and revolutionary technique of bitterness. Capitalism needs principally the virtue of justice in order that men may have their due; Communism needs principally the virtue of charity in order that men may dwell in unity, peace, and concord.

The Catholic Hierarchy of the United States has pointed out these two extremes. The group which forgets justice or capitalism, they described as those whose selfish interests disregard "the social purpose of property" with the result that "selfish interests or private profit rather than social well-being has succeeded in large measure in controlling the policies of governments, in directing finance and industry, and in subjecting labor policies to its own ends." The group which forgets charity or Communism -- they described as "designing agitators or cunning propagandists whose immediate interest is to create turmoil, bitterness, class conflict, and thus hasten a 'revolutionary situation.'"

Too often men approach the social problem by saying: "I am against Labor," or "I am against Capital," or "I hate the bankers," or "I hate the labor racketeers." A statement of this kind is a prejudice; it assumes that the saints are all on one side, and the devils are all on the other. Social justice does not mean hating the banker, nor hating the union organizer; it means seeking and loving the common good. No one class is always right, whether it be Capital or Labor, because society is not founded upon antagonistic classes, but upon their mutual functioning and correlation for the good of all. A great following could be built up in this country by a vicious attack on labor racketeers, just as a great following could be built up by an equally vicious attack on capitalists. But to do either is wrong, for it is to forget that a few union racketeers do not make unions wrong, any more than a few greedy capitalists make private property wrong. Our country must not be divided into two extreme classes at one another's throats, each seeking the death of the other; it must be built upon a justice and charity in which our individual rights and privileges are conditioned by the service of the common good. The forces of reaction which would continue the evils of capitalism can be just as wrong as the forces of anarchy which would pour out the baby with the bath. Let us not be fooled. There is a golden mean between the reaction of those who would retain the wrongs of an old order and the *revolution* of those who would totally destroy not only the abuse but even the use of that which is good. Somewhere, thanks to justice and charity, is a golden mean which does not destroy the past with its sacred accumulations of treasured wisdom, nor ignore the necessity of a peaceful change for an improved future existence. For example, one extreme error asserts that the capitalist has an absolute right to property and all its profits; the other extreme is that of Communism which asserts that the capitalist has no right at all to property, for all the rights belong to the workers who are entitled to all profits. In between both is the position of the Church which says that neither Capital nor Labor is entitled to *all* the profits, but *both* should share them because *both* have contributed to their creation.

Take another example: For some capitalists, a wage is just if the worker agrees to accept it, regardless of whether or not it be a living wage; for some labor racketeers, a wage is just if the capitalist agrees to pay it, regardless of whether his industry can bear it or not. In between these two extremes is the Catholic position that a wage is just when it takes into account three things: "the condition of the business," the "necessities of the workingman and his family," and the "economic welfare of all the people."

The golden mean will appeal neither to reactionaries nor revolutionists. It will seem traitorous to those who want capitalism condemned as intrinsically wicked, and it will seem cowardly to those who want to see Labor branded as irresponsible. It will be accused by the rich of being anti-capitalist; it will be accused by the workers as being anti-labor. It will appeal neither to those who hate bankers nor to those who hate labor organizers; but we trust it will appeal to identically the same people as those to whom the birth of Our Lord appealed: viz., "to men of good will." In other words, the spirit of our approach will be the Spirit of Justice and Charity, Who was born into our historical order nineteen hundred years ago, Who gave us a Gospel which gives no support to extremists who would exploit Labor nor to extremists who would violently dispossess Capital. Rather He taught us how to be capitalists without being exploiters, and how to be laborers without being Communists. And how did He show it better than at His birth, for incidental to the Incarnation was the union of the rich and the poor in the unity of His Divine Person. We must not make the sentimental mistake of thinking Our Lord was just a poor man; He was not just a laborer, nor a proletarian. He was a rich person who became a poor man. Such is the description of Him given by Saint Paul: "For you know the grace of our Lord Jesus Christ, that being rich He became poor for your sakes; that through His poverty you might be rich." Rich He was in His Divine nature because He was God, and Lord of heaven and earth. And yet despite that richness, He became poor, not only from an economic point of view but poor principally because He became man. That is poverty of the worst kind because it is a limitation. To the eternal confusion of Communists who teach that the rich were made to hate the poor and Labor was made to crush

Capital. He came to make both dwell in peace. He Who was born poor in a stable could have been born rich in a palace by the Tiber. Roman legions might have guarded Him at His birth, instead of an ox and an ass. It is this that makes Him the Supreme Reconciler of Capital and Labor, for no one would have expected that He Who made the gold of Caesar's throne would be born on a bed of straw; nor that He Who made the warmth of the sun, would be warmed by the breath of oxen; nor that He Who owned the earth would be homeless on the earth. Children were born in stables before, but never a Child Who might have been born in a palace. That fact alone makes His history unique. It is no wonder then that the world caught His Spirit, and that the first to come to His crib were the representatives of Capital and Labor -- the rich Magi and the poor Shepherds. There is no record that once there, they engaged in class conflict. Rather two things happened to them -- the rich lost their avarice, for they gave their wealth to the poor; the poor lost their envy, for they learned that there is another wealth than that which the rich men gave away. And on that day the world saw the Golden Mean between reaction and revolution.

As the Magi and the Shepherds left the crib, the Magi realized then, as never before, that the rich need the poor more than the poor need the rich. The destitute need the rich only in order to give them shoes for their feet, clothes for their bodies, a roof over their heads, food for their stomachs, and the necessities of a decent normal existence. But the rich need the destitute in order that they may have understanding in their minds, charity in their hearts, and the blessings of God on their lives. As Bossuet has put it: "You rich, make for yourselves friends of the poor; give and you shall receive; cast away your temporal blessings so that you may fill your empty treasure boxes with spiritual wealth... This is the only hope left for you, but there is that hope. You can receive privileges from the hands of the poor, and it is to them that the Holy Ghost sends you that you may obtain the graces bestowed by Heaven."

Just as that Babe called Magi and Shepherds to Himself and made rich and poor kneel in peace beside His crib, so the Church, which that Babe founded, calls both Capital and Labor to its communion rail to make them one because they eat the one Bread. Upon no other basis than that of the justice and charity of religion can enmities be abolished. It is no wonder then that those who most foster class hatred are those who are most opposed to the Babe of Bethlehem. As a Moscow daily puts it: "Christian charity which means kindness to all, even to one's enemies, is the greatest enemy of Communism." [1] Think of it -- Charity -- the enemy of Communism!

This means that the Saviour Who dies for His friends on a cross as a proof of love, is an enemy; that a saint who pours out Christ-like charity for the lepers, is an enemy; that a mother who forgives a hateful and unkind son, is an enemy; that a Stephen, being stoned, who prays: Forgive, "lay not this to their charge," is an enemy; that the charity

[1]*Pravda, March 30, 1934*

which inspires the noble love of the poor, the defense of the downtrodden, the caring for orphans and widows all because they are children of God, is an *enemy*! What a system! Charity, kindness, and forgiveness, an enemy! If charity is an enemy, then hatred, class struggle, and violence are virtues. And such is precisely the position of Communism. That is why it is so bent on inciting group against group, class against class, Capital against Labor, Labor against Capital, the poor against the rich, the rich against the poor, so as to keep society in such a state of rebellion, excitement and froth as to make the revolutionary overthrow of government possible, and the establishment in its place of a dictatorship over the proletariat.

We believe that justice is a better remedy than reaction and that charity is a better solvent than revolution. The solution of our problem is to be found in Him Who alone is the model of the rich and the model of the poor, the Exemplar of Capital and the Exemplar of Labor. To neither class does He belong exclusively, for He was neither rich nor poor: He was the rich poor man, and the poor rich man. He was the rich person Who voluntarily became a poor man, and therefore the One Who can call both to His crib and to His Church. As a matter of historical record, He is the only One Who ever walked this earth of ours of Whom both the rich and the poor, the masters and the servants, the employers and the employees, the kings and the carpenters, the capitalists and the laborers can say: "He came from our ranks; He is *one of our own*."

Contents

LIBERTY, EQUALITY
AND FRATERNITY

Chapter 1

Liberty

From an *economic* point of view, the three major programs offered for the ills of the modern world are: Liberalism, Communism and Christianity. In order that the presentation might be reduced to its simplest and clearest terms, we shall discuss them in relation to words so often seen engraved over the public buildings of France since the Revolution: "Liberty, Equality, and Fraternity."

The problem is: With which of the three shall we start to reconstruct a new social order? Liberalism says: "Begin with Liberty"; Communism says: "Begin with Equality"; and Christianity says: "Begin with Fraternity." In this chapter, we touch on liberalism.

By liberalism, we do not mean broadmindedness or progress, or tolerance. Rather by it is meant that system of thought which grew up in the eighteenth and nineteenth centuries, and which chose as its primary principle that which the word itself indicates, viz., liberty. But liberty for liberalism did not mean what it did traditionally. Liberty, correctly understood, is the right to choose between good things in order to develop the highest reaches of personality. For liberalism, liberty was not something *moral*, but rather something *physical*. It meant the right to do, to think or to say whatever one pleased without any regard for society, tradition, objective standards, or authority. This, as can readily be seen, is not liberty, but license. If liberty meant absence of all constraint, as liberalism said it did, then the policeman who refuses to permit me to drive through a red light is interfering with my liberty, which of course is sheer nonsense.

1. How did liberalism arise!
2. What were its principal doctrines?
3. *What is the attitude of the Church toward it?*

I.   *How did liberalism arise?*

Liberalism arose as a result of individualism. Individualism holds that every man has a right to make his own affirmations and a philosophy of life, without any reference to tradition or social organisms such as the Church or the State. This spirit of individualism had its roots deep in the fifteenth and sixteenth centuries. About that time the idea arose that religion should be a purely individual affair, that each man should be free to interpret his Bible as he saw fit, without any regard for a supreme court to judge the correctness of the interpretation. This idea, known as private interpretation of the Bible, was manifestly unsound, for a man left to himself is no more capable of drawing up his own religion than he is of drawing up his own astronomy. It was not long until individualism jumped out of the sphere of religion, into the realm of politics and economics. The merchants caught the spirit and said to the new religion:

"If you do not want a Church interpreting your Bible for you, neither do we want a Bible interpreting our business for us." Business is business and has nothing whatever to do with the moral and religious order. Just as I can think whatever I please, which shall be known as "freedom of thought"; just as I can do whatever I please, which shall be known as "freedom of expression," so I can run my business as I please; this spirit of individualism, applied to business and politics, became liberalism. It was not long until writers like Adam Smith in England attempted to justify it, by arguing that if the merchants were left free to run their business as they pleased, the maximum good of all would result. In France the scoffer Voltaire expressed the same idea negatively: "Any effort spent on instructing the servant and the shoemaker is a waste of time."

Liberalism, it can be readily seen, is based on a false idea of liberty. From the very beginning, it sought to discover a basis for individual freedom which would be free from all social constraint or what it called "state interference." In its form of "rugged individualism," it sought to limit state control to the barest minimum; it complained that the moral concepts of the Christian Ages, which gave each man a sufficiency within the framework of ethical principle, were inadequate for a new order, in which no limit should be placed on what a man could possess. The Christian concept that wealth is functional and is held in stewardship for society, was now considered as an undue limitation of an individual right to use wealth as one pleased.

During the Christian Ages, not the individual interest, but the common good, was the criterion of economics; sometimes the economic interest of an individual had to be sacrificed for the good of all. Under such a view, competition was controlled, speculation on a wide scale was prohibited, rates of interest were fixed, and feast days were compulsory. Under liberalism, on the contrary, the individual became of primary and the social of secondary importance. The next world had nothing to do with this, and if religion did enter into the scheme of life, it was only to bend men to the service of the liberalist idea. Tolerant it would be to religion, not always because religion was good, but because religious conflicts upset business. In a word, the new freedom meant the right to pursue wealth as an end in itself, and not, as it was traditionally, a means to both personal salvation and the enrichment of the social good. It produced what has been properly called an "acquisitive society whose whole tendency and interest and occupation is to promote the acquisition of wealth." Its battle cry we all know: Laissez-faire -- Keep your hands off." Let things alone -- Manufacture! Produce! Set the wheels of industry in motion! Enlarge your markets! Enrich your nation! Get wealth! More wealth! Even for the sake of wealth!"

II. *The three principal tenets of liberalism:*

a) The State must not interfere with business. The function of the State is purely negative, like a policeman's. A policeman does not intrude on our daily affairs except to protect us against trouble-makers; so too the State must not interfere with business, the expansion of its markets, the development of its resources, and the establishment of its own code of ethics based on profit, for to do so would be interference and the destruction of liberty.

b) No collective bargaining. Liberalism, leaving all things to uncontrolled competition, was opposed to all unions of wage earners. To defend this unsound position, liberalism argued: "Every man must be left free to make his own contract. But if workers enter a union, and the union bargains for hours and wages, the freedom of the individual to make his own contract is destroyed."

c) No interference with the absolute right of property. Edmund Burke arguing for liberalism said: "A magistrate has nothing to do with property; his interference is a violation of the property it is his office to protect." If one asserts that the right to property is absolute, then a merchant can not only make as much money as he pleases, but he can do with it whatever he pleases, even ignoring the common good; and the State which dares control in any way that wealth is accused of destroying liberty.

III. *What is the attitude of the Catholic Church to ward liberalism?*

The Church says all three tenets are wrong.

I. The State is not a policeman as liberalism holds, neither is it a nurse as Fascism and Communism hold.

The State exists for the *common good of all*, and not for the protection of a few privileged interests: "Civil Power is more than a mere guardian of law and order. While it is true that a just freedom of action should be left to individuals and families, it must be remembered that this principle is valid only as long as the common good is secured and there is no injustice... It is within the power of a ruler to benefit *every class* in the State ... but in a particular way the *interests of the poor*, and the State can do this without being accused of undue interference. Let it not be feared that solicitude of this kind will injure any interest; on the contrary, it will be to the advantage of all, for it cannot but be for the good of the commonwealth to rescue from its misery those on whom it so largely depends." [1]

2. Against liberalism which opposes collective bargaining, the Church argues that the workers have a right to organize. The Church frankly told the employers the real reason they were afraid to permit a union was not because they were afraid of violating freedom of contract, but because they were afraid of diminished profits if they had to pay higher wages. "Save the poor laborers," wrote Leo XIII, "from the cruelty of grasping speculators, who use human beings as mere instruments for making money." As regards the so-called freedom of contract, the Church contended that there is no freedom of contract if the worker has nothing, and the employer has everything. With only a hat in his hand and a wife and children to feed, he is *forced* under penalty of starving to accept whatever

---

[1] *Rerum Novarum*

wage is offered him. But by organizing into a union the workmen would have the force of their united corporate strength to bargain with the economic advantages of the employer. "Labor is not a commodity," said the same Pontiff. In order, therefore, to give him real bargaining power the Holy Father pleaded for labor unions "so organized and governed as to furnish the best and most suitable means for attaining what is aimed at, namely for helping each member to better his condition to the utmost, in body, soul and property." [2]

3. Man has not absolute control over the use of his property. Liberalism said: "I can earn as much wealth as I please, and I can do with it as I please." The Church answers: "You may accumulate as much money or property or capital, but you may not do with it whatever you please." And why? Because "the right to property is distinguished from its use." A man has a *right* to the wine which he has purchased by his labor, but he may not *use* it as he pleases, e.g., to intoxicate himself. "It is idle to contend that the right of ownership and its proper use are bounded by the same limits." [3] The use of the superfluities is subject to the common good. "No one is commanded to distribute to others that which is required for his own necessities and those of his household, nor even to give away what is reasonably required to keep up becomingly his condition in life; for no one ought to live unbecomingly. But when necessity has been supplied, and one's position

[2] Ibid.
[3] Ibid.

fairly considered, it is a duty to give to the indigent out of that which is over: 'That which remainest give alms.' [4]

Property then is not absolutely owned as liberalism said, nor is it to be confiscated by the proletariat as Communism holds. In between the two is the just balance which keeps the "natural right intact" [5] but nevertheless concedes that although the "state has no right to abolish it, it may control its use and bring it into harmony with the interest of the public good." [6]

One very important conclusion is to be drawn from the Church's condemnation of liberalism, namely, we must *avoid thinking that a change from the present order necessarily means the destruction of liberty*. Too often the liberty which the modern man seeks to defend is the liberty of individualism or liberalism, which is wrong. In rejecting Communism, for example, we must not fall into the error of defending the present order as right in all respects, nor call everyone a Red or a Communist because he is opposed to liberalism. The Church which condemns the Communism of today also condemned the liberalism of yesterday. Both destroy liberty, but in different ways. Liberalism destroyed liberty by dispensing the individual from social responsibilities; Communism and Fascism destroy liberty by enslaving the individual to the will of a dictator.

Before launching into a condemnation of any new order which disturbs the *status quo* of society on the grounds

[4]Ibid.
[5]Ibid.
[6] *Quadragesimo Anno.*

that it destroys liberty, let us make sure what liberty really means. There are two things it does not mean: the right to do whatever you please (liberalism) or the duty to obey the will of the dictator (Fascism and Communism). Liberty has something to do with the spiritual. Material things have no liberty, simply because they are material. Water has no liberty because it has no spirit; it must always seek its own level. In like manner, fire is a slave to heat and ice a slave to cold. But a man is free because he has a soul which being spiritual, intellectual, and immaterial, is not subject to the determining forces of matter.

Under no circumstances does freedom mean exemption from law. On the contrary, man enjoys liberty only on condition that he subject himself to a law. He is free to draw a triangle only on condition that he subject himself to its intrinsic law and draw it with three sides and not with thirty, in a fit of false broadmindedness. A man is free to fly only on condition that he respect the law of gravitation. In like manner, man is free to assert his personality, to own property, to earn profits only on condition that he recognize he is also a member of society, and therefore subject to the law of the common good. That is just where liberalism is wrong -- it is right in asserting man is free, but it is wrong in asserting that man may exercise that freedom apart from the good of humanity of which he is a part. He is free only on condition that he obeys the law which says he is a member of society and as such must seek the common good.

The liberty which the Church defends starts with the spiritual nature of man, and not with the absence of constraint, nor identity with the will of the dictator. Liberty based on the fact that man has a soul, is today a deserted shrine, but the Church declares that only when man returns to its homage will political and economic peace return. Start with that basic principle of the spiritual nature of man and it follows that the State will find its reason for being in securing to its citizens that freedom which is necessary for the perfection of the human personality. Because man is a natural being, the state will secure his intellectual liberty; because he is a moral being, the state will protect his freedom of conscience; because he is an economic being, the state will safeguard his ownership of productive property; because he is a social being, the state will protect his right of association... Because private property is the necessary foundation for individual liberty, it will be defended -- nay, if men will it, it shall be restored; because the family is the necessary training school of liberty, it will be protected in every possible way; because religion is a necessary discipline for liberty, it will not merely be tolerated, but the freedom of all forms of it which actually serve that end will be scrupulously respected." [7] But this is poles apart from the liberty of liberalism and the slavery of Communism.

The Church refuses absolutely to defend any social order which understands by liberty the right to do whatever one pleases, independently of the good of all.

[7]*Ross Hoffman, The Will to Freedom, p. 77.*

Private interpretation of business is wrong; freedom is not absence of constraint. Social control of individual business is not necessarily the destruction of human liberty. The freedom of liberalism in the eyes of the Church meant, and can only mean, the freedom to die of hunger. The Church has refused to accept as valid the arguments of liberalists that under its liberty a ditch digger could become the president of a bank, and a section hand could become the owner of a railroad. Against these cases, the Church has always retorted, that the few who did so rise to such positions of preëminence were no compensation for the millions who did not rise. It is no consolation for a hundred sheep to die by the teeth of wolves to know that the hundred and first of them will live in green pastures.

As far back as 1891, the Church warned the world that a false liberty which allowed every man to act as an isolated individual without any regard for the common good, would produce tremendous inequalities, viz., "concentration of wealth into the hands of the few," "the appropriation to capital of excessive advantages, claiming all the profits and products and leaving to the laborer the barest minimum to repair his strength." [8] And this is precisely what has happened. The privileged few became stabilized in wealth and a great mass became stabilized in poverty or at least as wage-earners. Liberalism did away with *political* inequalities by making all men equal before the law, but it produced tremendous *economic* inequalities or the concentration of wealth into the hands of the few.

[8] *Quadragesimo Anno.*

"It condemned the inequalities of the monarchical past but it glorified the inequalities of the industrial future." In a word, it begot capitalism, for capitalism, in a certain sense, is the heir of liberalism. It is these inequalities Communism hopes to cure. But before considering the Communist solution, which is the elimination of capitalism as something base, wicked, and seated in iniquity, it remains to ask this important question: What does the Church teach concerning capitalism?

Chapter II

Capitalism

The Church is opposed to any social system which interprets liberty as the right to do whatever one pleases. Such a system has been historically known as liberalism. In the economic order, it is known as capitalism, for capitalism was born of the spirit of liberalism. Everyone is familiar with the term "capitalism." Most of us have heard brilliant defenses of it by the vanishing race of "rugged individualists" or raucous and vicious attacks upon it by the Communists. Which is right? Is capitalism good or bad? What is the attitude of the Catholic Church toward capitalism?

The Church answers: Define your terms, for the answer depends upon what you understand by capital. ism. Capitalism may mean one of two things. It may mean broadly the private ownership of productive wealth for the sake of profit. In this sense the farmer who owns his land and tills it and then sells his corn and oats for profit is a capitalist; so is a baker who owns his own oven and shop and sells his bread to make money.

But capitalism may mean something more modern, namely, a "system by which great masses of wage-earners are so subject to capital in the hands of a few, that they are able to divert business and economic activity to their own arbitrary will and advantage, without any regard for the human dignity of workers, the social character of economic life, social justice or the common good."[1] Capitalism in this sense of the term includes not only yesterday's "competitive capitalism" [2] but even today's "monopolistic capitalism" [3] under which "immense power and despotic economic domination are concentrated in the hands of the few." [4]

Now that the terms are defined, the original question reappears: What is the attitude of the Catholic Church toward capitalism? The answer is: If you understand capitalism in the first sense, as the private ownership of productive wealth for profit, then the Church is not opposed to capitalism but in favor of it, for there is something good and stable about a society in which the farmer owns his land and the worker has a share in the "ownership or management or profits" of industry.

But if you understand capitalism in the second sense, i.e., a society in which a minority controls the means of production and claims all the products and profits and leaves to the laborer the barest minimum necessary to repair his strength and to ensure the continuation of his class," [5] then the Church is clearly and undeniably opposed to capitalism.

But why is the Church opposed to capitalism in the second sense of the term? (This is the sense in which we

[1]*Rerum Novarum.*
[2]Ibid.
[3]Ibid.
[4]Ibid.
[5]Ibid.

shall use the term capitalism from this point on.) The Church gives three reasons why it is opposed to capitalism: (1) Because it has concentrated wealth in the hands of the few; (2) Because it controls credit; (3) Because it seeks to dominate, economically, politically, and internationally.

(1) Capitalism has resulted in concentration of wealth into the hands of a few, and this concentration of power by these few far exceeds their ownership; more briefly, the few control more than they own. "It is patent that in our day not alone is wealth accumulated, but immense power and despotic economic domination is concentrated in the hands of the few, and those few are frequently not the owners, but only the trustees and directors of invested funds, who administer them at their good pleasure." [6] A proof of this pontifical critique of capitalism is that in 1929 only 2,458,049 individuals paid an income tax and in 1936 only 5,413,499. Ninety-two percent of the people in 1929 received less than $5,000 a year, whereas one-tenth of one percent of the wealthiest families had a total income as large as forty-two percent of the poorest families. Apropos of the power in the hands of the wealthy, let it be noted that the Senate Committee on Interstate Commerce reveals that a great railroad system was controlled by those who owned only two percent of the total invested capital.

(2) The Church is opposed to capitalism because as finance capitalism it permits credit to be concentrated in the hands of a few banks, thus creating additional

[6] *Quadragesimo Anno.*

servitude and dependence on the part of those who receive credit. "This power becomes particularly irresistible when exercised by those who, because they hold and control money, are able also to govern credit and determine its allotment, for that reason supplying so to speak, the life blood of the entire economic body, and grasping as it were, in their hands the very soul of production, so that no one dare breathes against their will." [7] That the Holy Father's protest against capitalism as controlling credit is justified one need only recall that the Congressional Record of the 72nd Congress reveals that eight banks in New York City in 1923 exercised control of 3,741 distinct corporations, such as insurance, public utility, transportation, manufacturing and the like.

(3) The Church is opposed to capitalism because its former "limitless free competition" has produced another great evil of capitalism, namely the "struggle for domination." This struggle for domination is threefold: (a) economic, (b) political, (c) international. (a) "First there is the struggle for dictatorship in the economic sphere itself -- a statement which is borne out by the fact that in 1933 less than 6oo firms owned over one half of the corporate wealth of the United States. (b) Political domination manifests itself in the fierce battle to acquire control of the state, so that its resources and authority may be abused in the economic struggle." [8] As far back as 1912 Woodrow Wilson said: "The government of the United

[7]Ibid.
[8]Ibid.

States at present is a foster child of the special interests." [9] The international domination is manifested "finally in the clash between the states themselves,[10] which is imperialism or the desire of economic dictators to extend their markets throughout the world even at the cost of human lives.

This criticism of the Holy Father concludes, "unbridled ambition for domination has succeeded the desire for gain; the whole economic life has become hard, cruel and relentless in a ghastly manner. Furthermore, the intermingling and scandalous confusing of the duties and offices of civil authority and of economics have produced crying evils and have gone so far as to degrade the majesty of the State." [11]

Now that the Church has given three reasons why it is opposed to modern capitalism, it is very much to the point to draw three very important conclusions: (1) The Communists' charge that the Church is the ally of capitalism, is absolutely false. Without any regard for truth, and with no other desire than to incite class hatred, it feeds minds on such slogans as the Marxian one: "Religion is the opium of the people." It repeats for the unsuspecting and the needy the lie of Lenin that "religion is a kind of spiritual intoxicant in which the slaves of capitalism drown their humanity and blind their desire for a decent human existence. [12] The fact is that the Church has never used religion to defend the rich or to put the

[9] *The New Freedom*, 1913, P. 58.
[10] *Quadragesimo Anno.*
[11] Ibid.
[12] *Novaya Zion, No. 28,* December 16, 1905.

working man to sleep, or to make him indifferent either to the ills of capitalism or the necessities of a decent human existence. Does the above criticism of capitalism read as if the Church were the ally of capitalism? Do these words, written in 1891 to the wealthy, read as if the Church were courting men's favor because they were wealthy! "Let the rich remember that to exercise profit for the sake of gain upon the indigent and the destitute, and to make one's profit out of the need of another, is condemned by all laws human and divine."[13] Not even millions given in charity by the capitalists to build libraries, research institutes, restore old monuments, or endow hospitals, says the Church officially, "can make amends for the open violation of justice." Going still further the Church teaches: "Neither must it be supposed that the solicitude of the Church is so occupied with the spiritual concerns of its children as to neglect their interests temporal and earthly. Its desire is that the poor should rise above poverty and wretchedness and should better their condition in life, and for this, it strives," always seeking to "save poor workers from the cruelty of grasping speculators, who use human beings as mere instruments for making money."[14]

When Communism says the Church is the ally of capitalism, it forgets this very important fact, namely, there is only one superficial and tiny resemblance between Catholicism and Communism, and that is, both condemn

[13] *Rerum Novarum.*
[14] Ibid.

the evils of capitalism. Instead of the Church being the ally of capitalism, it is Communism which is the ally of capitalism in carrying its abuses to the point where it substitutes a few red bureaucrats for a few capitalists. Communism is capitalism gone mad.

In the Church's criticism of capitalism, there is never a criticism of *persons* but only criticism of a system. But try to find a Communist attack upon capitalism which does not breathe hatred and class struggle in every line. Furthermore, the most vitriolic attacks by Communists upon capitalism have been made in the present day when the evils of capitalism are so marked. But the Church's calm, objective criticism was made as far back as 1891, in the very beginnings of capitalism, when it was enjoying its greatest successes and before its failures had become evident. When Communists say the Church is the friend of the capitalist and the enemy of the workingman, it would be well to remember that there are more solid arguments against the evils of capitalism in a calm Papal Encyclical, than one can find in a violent red sheet of propaganda; and the very arguments some Communists are using today against capitalism are taken from the Church documents already forty-seven years old, i.e., before the Communists had cut their baby teeth. Compared to the Encyclicals, the red attacks are but the wild ramblings of men who hate a class which oppresses more than they love a class which is oppressed. The Communists hate the capitalists more than they love the workers. They hate all the capitalists but they love only those workers who are willing to be duped by their propaganda. The rest to them are Fascists.

A second important fact to be noted is that capitalism in the eyes of the Church is not identical with *private ownership*." Is it not deplorable that the right of private property," writes the Holy Father, "defended by the Church, should so often have been abused to defraud the workingman of his wages and his social rights?" [15] It is important to understand this distinction, for Communism attempts to make this equation by asserting that both the Church and capitalism believe in private property; therefore, it concludes the Church is the friend of capitalism. No! The Church defends the right to private property, but not the *abuse* of that right. The *right* to property, in the eyes of the Church, is not identical with the right to use property as *one pleases*, but rather the right to use it for the *common good*. It is absolutely false for anyone to say, "I can do whatever I will with my industry because it is my own." The owner's right is in part conditioned by its use, for without justice there is no absolute right, not even the authority of a dictator, whether he be Fascist or Communist. The Church affirms against the Communist the natural right of a man to own property, either for purposes of production or consumption, but it denies against capitalism that its rights to profits is prior to the human right to a living wage. The virtue of justice intervenes against both capitalism and Communism. Against capitalism, justice protests against capitalism's claim to do with property whatever one

[15] *Divini Redemptoris.*

pleases; against Communism, justice protests Communism's claim to confiscate all property in the name of the red leaders. Justice will tolerate neither those capitalists who assert an absolute right to property, nor those Communists who deny there is any right at all.

This brings us to our third and final observation concerning the relation of the Church and Communism to capitalism. Communism says that capitalism is intrinsically wicked, because it admits the right to own private property and the use of it for the sake of profit. The Church answers: "It is not vicious of its nature" and then proceeds to make a distinction between the *right* to a thing and the *use* of the thing. The right may be good; the use may be wrong. A policeman has a right to his gun, but he may not use it to shoot babes in arms. Communists say because some policemen abuse the right to their guns: "Take all guns away from all policemen and give them to us and we will be your O.G.P.U." The Church says: "Deprive only those policemen of their guns who abuse their right to have them." In like manner, Communism says, because some capitalists abuse the right to property, therefore destroy it. The Church answers: "No. Do not destroy a lawful right, but reform the abuses for the "misuse or non -- use of ownership does not destroy nor forfeit the right of ownership." [16] To put it all very simply, Communism finding rats in the barn, burns the barn. The Church drives out the rats.

Furthermore, while protesting against these evils in

[16] *Quadragesimo Anno*

capitalism, and while pleading to the State to use its power to defend the workingman and the poor, the Church is not blind to the fact that there may be evils on the other side. Labor must not lay the flattering unction to its soul that all the evils are on one side and all the good on the other. Labor too needs a reminder: "Religion teaches the laboring man to carry out honestly and well all the equitable agreements freely made, never to injure capital nor to outrage the person of the employer; never to employ violence in representing his own cause, nor to engage in riot and disorder; and to have nothing to do with men of evil principles who work among the people with artful promises and raise foolish hopes which usually end in disaster and repentance when too late." [17]

In conclusion, these are the two important teachings of the Church. (1) It is unequivocally opposed to the evils of capitalism. Communism joins the Church in its protest and in this Communism is right, but Communism is wrong in its reform which is the abolition of private productive property by violent confiscation. (2) The Church in defending the right of private property does not defend its abuse, which is capitalism.

That is why Communism and Catholicism have two entirely different solutions for the problem of inequality produced by the evils of capitalism. Communism proposes to solve inequalities by confiscation and dispossession and collectivism, the Church by legislation and *distribution*. A parable will make it clear.

[17] *Rerum Novarum.*

In a certain rural section of the country, there are a dozen farmers selling eggs to a city. Partly by hard work, partly by dishonesty, partly by unjust trade practices, one farmer finally controls practically the whole egg market, while the other eleven farmers are reduced to a state where most of them have to work for the monopolist, and a few go on relief. This inequality in the egg business needs a solution. How solve the problem?

The Communist solution is this: First, they send one of their organizers among the eleven farmers, inciting them to upset the delivery wagon of the capitalist, at the same time organizing legal groups to defend violence on the grounds of liberty. Next, they throw stones at the hens on their nests in order to disturb production, all the while telling the farmers about the big goose eggs which the Socialist hens lay at the command of their beloved Stalin. After the Communist organizer has developed class hatred between one farmer and the other, and in general, has disturbed both hens and eggs and their distribution, he then, "acting as the vanguard of the masses," seizes all the hens and all the eggs of the twelve farmers. The farmer who owned most of the hens and the eggs naturally resists, but he is "liquidated," which is the Communist word for murder. Two or three of the eleven do not like such violence and plead against bloodshed, so they are called "Fascists" and "Trotskyites" and sent to a lumber camp. Then the Communist organizer says to all the farmers who are left, "The problem of equality is solved. You all own equally; there are no more selfish classes, for I am your

Dictator and I own all, in the Dictatorship of Eggdom." Then to prove they are equal, he makes an omelet out of all their eggs and invites them to dinner.

The solution of the Church is quite different. Starting with the same fact of inequality, it says to the twelve farmers: "You are all members of a farmer association called the 'Grange.' Last week you elected farmer Jones as your president. He is charged to seek your common good, just as the State seeks the common good of its citizens. He will do several things for you to adjust the inequalities. (1) Permit you eleven to form an organization to protect your rights. (2) He may by his authority break up the monopoly of the one who now controls the egg-market and specify what is 'licit and what is illicit in ownership, and even 'adjust ownership to meet the needs of the public good,' of all of you. (3) He may also, through wise legislation, if you do not wish to go in the egg business yourself, permit you to work for the former monopolist, but he will give you a 'share in the ownership, profits or management of his business.

"But in no case will he use violence, permit you to call one another names, nor will he make an omelet for you. He believes in liberty, and fully realizes the fact that some of you like your eggs boiled, others fried and others prefer to have them raw."

The Church believes in putting the eggs in as many baskets as possible, for only when a man is master of the way his eggs are to be cooked, can he be called the master also of his soul. Communism, on the contrary, puts all the eggs in one basket. Instead of allowing each man to cook his own eggs according to his taste, Communism makes an omelet. How poor Communism's omelet really is, is the burden of the next chapter.

Chapter III

Equality

How begin reconstructing a social order? Liberalism and Capitalism said: "Start with liberty understanding liberty as the absence of constraint." Capitalism had its liberty and it produced unjustified in equalities, the concentration of wealth and power in the hands of a few, and the general impoverishment of the masses. It was only natural for another system to arise offering to heal inequalities by preaching equality, and such is Communism. There is something good about Communism and that is its protests against the injustices begotten by liberalism. But two very important cautions must be kept in mind: firstly, Communism is not alone in protesting against injustices; all who believe in virtue and they are legion -- make exactly the same protest. Leo XIII registered a more coherent and objective protest against certain evils of the industrial order than Communism, even with its violent hatred of capitalism. Secondly, we must not be fooled by believing that because the protests of Communism are right, therefore their *reforms* are right. Cutting off one's head is a remedy for toothache, and so is Communism a remedy for capitalism, but both are bad remedies. The proper way to judge a platform is not by its negations, but by its affirmations. Because Communists hate the rich is not a proof that they love the poor; it may only mean that they want to be rich themselves. I can protest against the bad odor of dead lilies without being madly in favor of perfume. If then, we are to understand the value of Communism as a solution, we must judge it, not by its protests, but by its reforms.

The reform suggested by Communism is conditioned by the revolutionary overthrow of our government and our civilization. Such is indeed the warning recently issued by the American bishops: "Unhampered by any fixed moral principles, Communists would hasten the collapse of the structure of our government, calculating that they will be beneficiaries as the leaders of the new order. If for the moment they are keeping their activities largely under cover, it is because they are biding their time awaiting the hoped for collapse."

In order that there may be no false presentation of the Communist position, we shall allow Communism to speak for itself through its official Program published and distributed by the Workers Library Publishers for the Communist Party of the United States. The three basic ideas in the Program are: 1. The tremendous inequalities in the world today are due to capitalism which throws the principal emphasis on property, and which, by its very nature, divides men into classes—those who have and those who have not -- or the exploiting and the exploited class. "The characteristic feature of the capitalist society which arose on the basis of commodity production is the monopoly of the most important and vital means of production by the capitalist class and big land lords; the exploitation of the wage labor of the proletariat which, being deprived of the means of production, is compelled to sell its labor power."[1] 2. Since the ownership of productive property is the basis of inequalities and classes, it follows that if the capitalists are deprived of their productive property by putting it all into the hands of the collectivity, inequalities will be done away with and a classless class established. "The abolition of private property and the disappearance of classes will do away with the exploitation of man by man." "After abolishing private property in the means of production and converting them into social property Communist society will abolish the class division of society." [2] 3. Naturally a society in which the means of production are privately owned will not willingly surrender its property. Therefore the workers must organize, and violently and by force take the property away from the owners, overthrow the government which fosters productive property, and liquidate all those who resist and who are allied with the old regime. In order to understand the language used by the Communists in their Program remember that "Proletariat" means labor or wage-earner and "bourgeois power" means any government which is non-Communistic, e.g., our own. The tendency now is to use Fascist instead of "bourgeois" in order not to alienate the middle class. "Proletarian revolution signifies the forcible invasion of the proletariat into the domain of property relationships, the

---

[1] *Communist Program, p. 11.*
[2]*Ibid., Pp. 12, 30.*

expropriation of the expropriating class."[3]

In order to make it clearer, let us ask this Official Program a series of questions, and seek the answers verbatim in the Program itself.

1. Must there be a revolution before Communism can be established, and what does it imply?

Ans. Yes. The revolution demands the forcible nationalization of all productive capital. "Between Capitalist society and Communist society a period of revolutionary transformation intervenes. ... Proletarian revolution, however, signifies the forcible invasion of the proletariat into the domain of property."[4]

2. What will happen to the capitalists whom the Communists always call "exploiters"?

Ans. "The characteristic feature of the transition period as a whole is the ruthless suppression of the resistance of the exploiters."[5]

3. What will happen to Church lands, productive property, industry, transportation, communication services, and big housing property?

Ans. The Official Program uses the same word in relation to all of them, namely, "confiscation." It then adds that confiscation applies to "all property utilized in production belonging to large landed estates, such as buildings, machinery, and other inventory, cattle,

[3]Communist Program, p. 35
[4]Pp. 34. 35.
[5]P. 36.

enterprises for the manufacture of agricultural products (large flour mills, cheese plants, dairy farms, fruit and vegetable drying plants, etc.)."[6]

4. What will happen to the middle classes who are not sympathetic to the Communist revolution and to those who are in favor of land owners?

The answer is suppression. "The Proletariat must neutralize the middle strata of the peasantry and merci lessly suppress the slightest opposition on the part of the village bourgeoisie who ally themselves with the land owners."[7]

5. What will happen to the liberal left-wingers and the intelligentsia who refuse to go the full way of the Communist revolution?

The Program calls for "ruthlessly suppressing every counter-revolutionary action on the part of the hostile sections of the intelligentsia."[8]

6. Why is violence necessary for a Communist revolution?

The Program answers because it enables Communism to get rid of those who oppose it. Think of how much bloodshed there is hidden in these following lines, as the history of Russia has so well proven to be true. "The mass awakening of Communist consciousness, the cause of socialism itself, calls for a *mass change of human nature* which can be achieved only in the course of the practical movement, in revolution. Hence, revolution is not only necessary because there is no other way of overthrowing

[6]P. 41.
[7]P. 49.
[8]P. 48.

the *ruling* class, but also because, only in the process of revolution is the *overthrowing* class able to purge itself of the dross of the old society." [9]

7. What is the official attitude of Communism toward religion?

"One of the most important tasks of the cultural revolution affecting the wide masses is the task of systematically and unswervingly combating religion -- the opium of the people." [10]

8. Does the Communist revolution propose to seize government power and to overthrow our armies, our police, and our courts!

Ans. The Program calls for their "violent overthrow." "The conquest of power by the Proletariat is the violent overthrow of bourgeois power, the destruction of the capitalist state apparatus (bourgeois armies, police, bureaucratic hierarchy, the judiciary, parliaments, and so forth)." [11]

Such is Communism. Its good points are that it attempts to deal with the real problem of inequality and protests rightly against certain forms of exploitation practiced by some capitalists. But because men complain against the ravages of typhoid fever, it does not follow that they are doctors, nor because Communism protests against social injustices, does it follow that Communists know how to deal with the problem. The following analogy will show its basic general failure: If two boys were about to start a fight over a few marbles, the normal onlooker would not

9 P. 52.
10 P. 53
11 P. 36.

goad them on to hate one another with greater fury, in order that he might seize their marbles: rather he would seek to avoid the conflict and arrive at a peaceful equitable solution. This analogy suggests the extremist character of the Communistic solution. Quite apart from the bloodshed, civil war, and hate, inspired by its revolutionary overthrow of the existing order, it attempts to cure over possession by dispossession. A more sane solution would be distribution, as we shall indicate later. Because there are moths in the woolens is no reason for burning the woolens, it is only a reason for buying mothballs.

Apart from the chaos incident to the overthrow of the existing order, there are two serious defects in the Communist ideal of equality and the classless class: 1. It purchases equality at the terrible cost of freedom. 2. It really does not destroy inequality, but creates a new and worse kind, namely the inequality of privilege. In the language of the Church the first defect of Communism is its destruction of freedom: "Communism strips man of liberty, robs human personality of all its dignity and removes all moral restraints that check the eruptions of blind impulses. There is no recognition of any right of the individual in his relation to collectivity; no natural right is accorded to human personality which is a mere cog-wheel in the Communist system. ... Communism recognizes in the collectivity the right, or rather, unlimited discretion, to draft individuals for the labor of the collectivity with no regard for their personal welfare; so that even violence could be legitimately exercised to dragoon the recalcitrant against their wills." [12]

Facts justify the Church's contention that Communism destroys liberty in its attempt to create equality. Just suppose a doctor set about to establish equality of all the members of the body so that the legs would no longer exploit the feet by walking on them, so that the tongue would no longer exploit the stomach by getting all the taste and the stomach none, so that the eye would no longer exploit the brain by seeing all the colors, leaving the brain only images. Upon what condition could the doctor make every member equal? Only on condition that he should destroy the function and the purpose of each organ. In like manner, Communism establishes equality by suppressing liberty, by making man merely a cog in the productive machinery of the State. Suppress function in the body and you destroy the organ; suppress freedom in the citizen and you destroy the citizen. Human beings are not machines, and to force everyone to think as the dictator thinks and to do what the dictator commands may make for economic equality, but at a cost which none of us is willing to pay, namely the surrender of our freedom. To force men into a mold is the great defect of all totalitarian states, whether Fascist or Communist, for in this the two agree: the citizens are subject to the will of the dictator. Liberalism understood liberty as the absence of constraint and produced unjustified inequality; Communism understands equality as common ownership of the means

[12] *Divini Redemptoris.*

of production under a dictatorship, and destroys freedom. Communism thinks men are equal if they all share according to their needs and capacities in economic wealth, but slaves who are well cared for by the slave -- owners are equal in the same sense. Neither are free so long as their wills are subject to a dictator in those matters which make man a man. Equality is not a political concept, in the sense that all individuals have the same racial characteristics; it is not an *economic* concept, in the sense that all who share the same cake are equal. It is rather a *spiritual* concept, in the sense that all men are members of a common humanity and therefore are entitled to the common heritages of civilization without the arbitrary penalties of a power which would make man exist for the State instead of the State for man. So long as the workers are at the mercy of that dictator, so long as the dictator can compel reluctant obedience of the worker by force, terror, **O.G.P.U.** propaganda and blood purges, so long as the workers themselves are unable to protest against dictatorship save at the cost of grave personal injury, imprisonment or death, so long as they must court the favor of that dictator by parades, demonstrations and "long live the workers' friend," so long as they are exiled or shot because they insist on their right to worship God according to the dictates of their consciences -- despite all their successful Five-Year Plans, their great army, their new bathrooms and radios, their new luxuries from night clubs to subways—they can hardly be said to be free! They may all be equal as workers, but so are the prisoners in a work house! It is better to be poor and free than to have one's stomach full and not be able to call one's soul one's own. What doth it profit a worker if he has all his material wants satisfied, if he cannot protest against a regime which would deny him the spiritual when his day's work is done! Man is more than a "worker"; if he were only this, he would be no different from a tractor. The cogs in a machine are all equal in the sense that they serve according to their capacities and are served by other cogs according to their needs, but man is not a cog in the machinery of the State regardless of how well he is oiled by propaganda. He has also a soul whence his freedom is derived. Equality demands then, not that he have as much as any other worker in Russia, but that he have the same *rights* as any other man in the world and that means the right to *dissent* with dictatorship because he is *rational*; the right to protect his freedom of conscience against State religions and State atheism, because he is *moral*; the right to protect his personality in ownership of productive property because he is *economic*; and the right to form associations, political and religious because he is a social being. Such equality implies freedom, and any system which thinks it can make men free after it makes them prosperous is beginning at the wrong end. Rather begin with the right kind of freedom and then they will be prosperous.

That Communism in its attempt to destroy inequalities, destroyed liberty, is proven by facts taken from a country where the Communist Party has been in power for twenty years: 1. Under Communism there is no freedom of confessional liberty, i.e., one may not carry on any kind of propaganda for religion nor teach religion to children in groups of over three. Article 124 of the Constitution does not grant religious liberty in the sense that one may propagate religion. The right to anti-religious propaganda is reserved to the State. That such is the meaning of the article; we refer to Yaroslavsky, the leader of the anti-God campaign, who, in his work, *Stalin's Constitution and the Problem of Religion,*[13] is writes: "The Constitution grants us the right of anti-religious propaganda and we will use it in order to strike a more formidable blow at religion."

2. There is no freedom of press, freedom of speech, or freedom of assembly under Communism, for Article 125 of the Soviet Constitution allows the use of the press which belongs to the State, only on condition that it be used to strengthen the socialist system." And that this interpretation is correct, we refer to the *Pravda*, the official Communist organ of Moscow, which under date of June 22, 1936, says that anyone attempting to "undermine the socialist system will not receive a sheet of paper, nor will ever be permitted to pass through the door of a printing shop, nor will he find a room, a hall, or a corner to pour out his poisonous words." Would we say we had freedom of the press in the United States if every newspaper, radio, and writer had to bolster one of the political parties of the United States and would be declared "an enemy of the people" if they did not? Would

---

[13] Moscow Ogiz and Gaiz State Anti-religious Publishing Co. 1936.

we say we possessed freedom if those who dissented with the President were shot without trial? Would we say we had freedom of the press and speech in America if we were permitted to have only one party, and all dissidents, who felt there should be another party, were killed or sent to a concentration camp, where they learned the wisdom of keeping their collective mouths shut? Would we say that we had freedom of speech in America if thirty-five experts of our Department of Agriculture were shot without trial, because they opposed the party, as actually happened in Russia in 1933? Would we say we had liberty in the United States if the President, within the space of three months, executed the governors of our forty-eight States; and yet this is precisely what the "beloved Stalin" did for he executed the heads of the Republics of the Soviet Union in three months.

This criticism is true of any totalitarian State, Fascist or Communist. The curious fact about it all is that here in America we will allow Communists to attack our President and our government, a crime for which they would be shot in Russia.

3. There is only one party allowed in Russia, namely the Communist Party, and the nomination of all candidates for election belongs to the Communist Party. Such is Article 141 of the Constitution. This means there is no real freedom of election; the people can in theory choose between candidates of the one party, they cannot choose between parties. In fact, they cannot even choose between candidates, for in the last general election there

were not more than 30 districts out of 1,143 in which they had more than one candidate. They can agree who will be elected in the party, but not by secret ballot -- only by raising hands; they dare not disagree with the party, and in this, the Communists and Fascists agree: millions vote and have no voice in government. Communism makes much of its secret ballot, but the secrecy of the ballot does not matter; what does matter is whether the secret ballot allows you to choose between parties, policies, principles. The last election in Russia was a shotgun plebiscite and reveals unity of assent to Communism, but a unity under compulsion. A hundred percent electoral victory for Stalin does not demonstrate that everyone believes in Communism, it only demonstrates that Stalin is still strong enough to make his slaves vote for him. Without a choice between recognized opposition, all the secret ballots in the world are a farce and are but the dramatized acquiescence in decisions made in the single mind of the dictator which is much more secret than any ballot box. Add to this the fact that less than 1 1/2 percent of the entire population of Russia belongs to the Communist Party, which alone possesses the "right to nominate candidates," and you get a true picture of the 1 1/2 percent of the population dominating the 98 1/2 percent. This they call "democracy."

4. There is no freedom to strike in Russia. This may come as a surprise to Americans who are so familiar with the Communist's passion to incite strikes and violence here in America, but the fact is that Article 131 forbids the

strike under penalty of becoming "an enemy of the people." They throw wrenches into everyone else's machine here, and subject one to the criminal code if one throws a wrench into their machine. This Article 131 is nothing but a republication of the "*Declaration* of the Central Council of Workers (1926) which states: "The strikes are held to be a counterrevolutionary act," and it is well to remember that in six months of 1937 over six hundred were shot in Russia for "counter-revolutionary acts."

The true picture presents itself if you recall that there is only one boss in all Russia, and that is the State. Hence you cannot go elsewhere to get a job, once the State writes across your passport "disorganizer of labor." It is quite true that not all bosses in America are saints, but even when they are not, they exercise only economic rights over their workers, i.e., what they shall receive, the hours they shall work, and the conditions under which they labor. But in Russia, the State, which is the sole employer, exercises not only economic rights over the workers, but even *juridical* rights, i.e., the employer has the power of life and death over the worker, and if that is not the end of liberty, then we might just as well throw away our dictionaries.

There is no need to multiply the obvious conclusions: Any system, Fascist or Communist, which attempts to secure equality by making the dictator the master of man, destroys freedom. What chances have any dissatisfied group of men of hiring a hall in Germany or Russia or Italy to criticize Hitler or Stalin or Mussolini? How long would

States protest the picketing of the Kremlin to denounce Soviet shipments of oil to aid Mussolini in Ethiopia, as actually happened? How much chance has an American book, article or newspaper criticizing a single European dictator of finding its way into their countries? A totalitarian State, either Fascist or Communist, can do nothing else by its nature than subjugate otherwise free men into the yokes made by its dictators. What is more, it forces them, by the dope of propaganda and the terror of secret police, to such an extent that they no longer know they are being forced. They are humbugged by their press into believing that outside their country there is nothing but starvation and ruin. The list of so-called "liberties" mentioned in the new Soviet Constitution in Chapter 10, from universal suffrage to guaranteed privacy of letters, are all subject to the limiting clause "in so far as the Communist Party permits." This means these liberties do not belong to man as man, but only as State-given temporary privileges. Therefore the State can take these privileges away. Would we say we had liberty in America if either the Democratic or the Republican Party should take away our right to the privacy of correspondence!

Not all the propaganda in the world can drown the plain fact: equality under Communism means only the equal duty to glorify the dictator, but never to be free to dissent. The only freedom, under a dictatorship, is the freedom to cease complaining. Under a democracy to complain against a banker or a president is sometimes the road to public office, but to whisper a word against a dictator is the road to death, without even the consolation of a public martyrdom.

II. The second judgment against Communism is that instead of establishing economic equality, it creates new inequalities and levels its majority to poverty. "It would open the door to envy ... and instead of the ideal equality of which so much is said would, in reality, be the leveling down to the same condition of misery and dishonor." [14] First of all there is the difficulty of defining equality under Communism. It prides itself on equality because it gives to each according to his toil. But what does equality mean? Equality cannot be defined because "equality of reward has only a subjective meaning, whereas wage schedules, occupational requirements, the recruitment of labor, and the selection of managers and officials are objective decisions. The two cannot be reduced to a common denominator. Thus if money incomes are equal how shall the pleasure and pain of the effort expended be equalized? How many hours in a coal mine are equal to how many hours in a commissar's office? If wages are proportioned to the product, the coal miner will get a larger return in a good mine than in a poor mine. If he is deprived of this economic advantage, then wages cannot be equalized with productivity. If opportunity is equal, then achievements will be unequal. For ability is not equal. If ability is equalized -- say by putting a good farmer on poor land and a poor farmer on good land -- then opportunity is not equal." [15]

[14] *Rerum Novarum*
[15] Walter Lippmann, The Good Society, p. 77. Little, Brown & Company.

Apart from this inconsistency, there is this evident fact: it is quite true that Communism does away with the inequalities of wealth because the State owns all the means of production, but in its place, it has created the inequalities of privilege. There are no more big bankers, but there are red leaders; there are no more capitalists, but there are commissars. The president of a great automobile corporation in America may not own an automobile, but because of the power his office gives, a commissar can enjoy the privilege of thousands of cars. In like manner, Communism has done away with the aristocracy of money, but it has not done away with the new aristocracy of privilege. And how could it be otherwise in a regime where *ownership* is distinct from administration. Under Communism, the *ownership* of the means of production is common, i.e., it belongs to the workers, but the *administration* of that ownership resides in the hands of the leaders. Thieves who rob a bank own the loot in common, but the quarrels begin when the ringleaders divide the spoils. Then everyone wants to divide. And so it is with Communism. It begins by the violent confiscation of wealth, but everyone knows that if the leaders were disposed to steal from the capitalists in the beginning, why should they not be disposed to steal from the workers in the end? Do not we read daily in the press about purges in Russia? Communism said that private property is the basis of all injustice and exploitation and that when private property is done away with by socialization, society would be harmonious. This has not been the fact. The enforced transfer of title to property works no magic in the hearts of men, and can no more revolutionize human behavior than wearing a neighbor's hat. Selfishness, injustice, greed are not in *things*, they are in *souls*, and when Communism rejected religion it cut off from itself all possibility of regenerating society. If socializing property did away with injustices we would never hear, as we do, of profiteering by red leaders, of profiteering by farm managers, and of raids on the public treasury, nor would we hear of Stalin first killing his enemies and then killing his friends.

Starting a new order by violent confiscation and murder as Communism starts its new order, cannot make for peace. Can injustice be the road to Paradise? Can life come from death, love from hate, peace from violence? Confiscating the means of production and socializing them does not do away with the passion for property, any more than the stealing of a man's clothes does away with the shame of nakedness. There is something to be envied under capitalism, namely, wealth, and there is still something to be envied under Communism, namely, who will have charge of it? Under capitalism, it is personal wealth that produces inequalities, under Communism, it is the personal control of that confiscated wealth which produces the new inequalities. The struggle for wealth under capitalism, as Mr. Lippmann suggested, has became a struggle for power under Communism. Regardless of how loud one prattles about "comradeship" there has still been found no way of making Communists economic eunuchs, absolutely devoid of the passion of wealth, and therefore workers, just as content to sit in a ditch as in the Kremlin.

For factual evidence of inequalities under Communism, let us again quote Communist sources. Red leaders receive commonly salaries of 12,000 rubles a month [16] and are always served first in the stores, [17] whereas the average pay of a Russian worker for 1936 was only 225 rubles a month, and a pair of shoes costs between 180 and 200 rubles, or almost a month's salary. [18] Engineers often earn eighty to one hundred times as much as an unskilled worker. [19]

Inequalities apply not only to salaries but to the necessities of life, so that while the red leaders and the army are well-fed, no less an authority than Soulimov, the President of the Council of the People's Commissars, stated: "Everything is at a very low level, save the prices which are exorbitant." [20]

John T. Whittaker, the Moscow correspondent of the *Chicago Daily News*, figured out how much shoes cost in Russia in terms of American exchange which is five rubles to the dollar. A pair of shoes in Russia, which sells for 220.5 rubles, and is equal to a $3 American shoe in quality, would cost in American money $44.10. Even if one did have money, it would not always be easy to find the necessities. "For weeks, and even for months," says an

[16] Za. Ind., December 14, 1935: October 16, 1935.
[17] Ibid., February 6, 1936.
[18] Sovietskaia Torgevlin, Nos. 99, 110--1936.
[19] The New International, February 1936.
[20] Pravda, July 31, 1936.

official Russian page, "sugar, soap, matches, salt, tea, tobacco, etc. were not on sale in the Dnepropetrovsky region and in many regions in Western Siberia. In Central Russia, no sugar was available for two months. In Crimea out of 559 grocery shops investigated 287 had no sugar; 185 no salt and 214 no flour."[21] It would be a safe guess, however, that one could find a picture of Stalin even when one could not find bread. At a party meeting, December 7, 1936, the name Stalin was used 57 times. The word "great" was applied to him 18 times, the word "beloved" 8, and the word "genial" 9.

Harold Denny, Moscow correspondent for the *New York Times*, summarized Russia after twenty years of Communism as follows in *Time*, Sept. 27, 1937.

Wages: "... In twenty years the revolution has made so little progress toward emancipation if it has not, indeed, retrogressed—that the Soviet worker is among the most exploited in the world. ... And the State has proved that it can be as hard a taskmaster as any capitalist boss and can enforce its will with a police power infinitely stronger than any coal or iron police or venal "company' sheriff in the United States.

" 'Surplus value', which is one of the foundation stones of Marx's philosophy -- the amount that the worker gives the employer in labor above what is received -- is exacted in the Soviet system too. In Russia that surplus value is being used to extend capital construction, to build up a military establishment, and to maintain a swollen army of

[21] *Investia*, February 14, 1936.

bureaucratic functionaries who probably consume more of the workers' toil than the proprietor class in capitalism. ... Inefficiency holds down the wages that the Soviet can pay -- and it like any capitalist employer must make a profit or go out of business -- and enormously increases the cost of everything the Soviet citizen buys. It makes [the worker's] real wage extremely low. And the quality of almost everything he buys is so bad that the goods could not compete with capitalistically produced goods for a minute in any free market."

Freedom: "Conceding what I believe to be true -- that the Soviet regime is sincerely doing all it can materially for the people as a whole -- it has, nevertheless, utterly eradicated freedom of expression on any except the most innocuous topics. ... The result is an intellectual servility of sycophancy, a hypocrisy that is simply degrading."

Employment: "There is no unemployment now simply because there is a constant labor shortage. ... The labor shortage has been made more acute by the fact that inefficiency, bureaucracy, and the prevalence of parasitic functionaries have greatly reduced labor productivity. Foreign engineers have estimated that four times as many persons, or more, are required under Soviet conditions to turn out a given production as are required in the United States... But industry is going badly from top to bottom. ... The Soviet has given industry everything in materials, but has failed to give the most important thing of all-freedom to executives to use their own initiative and to make their own decisions, confident that if a high percentage of decisions are correct an occasional error will be forgiven. In the Soviet, an executive error may land a good man in prison under terrible charges of wrecking...."

William H. Chamberlin, who spent twelve years in Russia, makes a comparison of what the average American worker can buy as contrasted with the Soviet worker. The basis of the comparison is the U. S. Bureau of Labor Statistics for 1933 -- a depression year -- with the official figures as reported in the *Moscow Daily News* For a month's salary the Soviet worker can get but 19 pounds of butter and the American worker can buy 240 pounds. The Soviet worker can buy 90 pounds of sugar and the American can buy 1,120 pounds. The Soviet worker can buy 40 pounds of first-grade beef with his month's salary and the American can buy 200 pounds. In other words in one of the worst years of our depression, the American could buy from five to twelve times that which the Soviet wage of 1935 could buy. Chamberlin also says that after returning to Moscow he read off to his Russian friends a list of the food stuffs that were given to the unemployed in Milwaukee as part of their relief, and the Soviets said no worker could ever eat like that; the list sounded like the ration of a red leader. [22]

Sir Walter Citrine, General Secretary of the Trades Union Congress and President of the International Federation of Trades Unions, after a long studied trip

[22] *Collectivism*, pp. 74 and 85.

through Russia, in his book, *I Search for Truth in Russia*, states that the poor on relief in America, Eng. land and France receive in benefit more than the Soviet workers receive in wages. [23] This idea is confirmed by Norman Thomas, the Socialist leader, in an article in the *Socialist Call*, June 5, 1936, which he wrote after his return from Russia. He found that the Russian peasant and worker live under the strictest passport system in the world, that they have no right of free association, and that their average monthly salary in American money is $46. One of the very interesting personal experiences of the tragic lot of the Soviet workers which explodes all the untruths of propaganda is the book of Andrew Smith entitled *I was a Soviet Worker*. For sixteen years he and his wife were active members of the Communist Party in the United States. They swallowed whole the Communist propaganda about the happiness of the workers, went to Russia with a delegation of American workers, visited the factories and schools and hospitals which the Intourist guide permitted them to see, were feasted and feted, met at stations with bands and, in their own words, "looked toward the Soviet Union as the beacon light of hope for suffering humanity." On returning to America they gave their life's earnings to the Communist Party, went back to Russia, but there were no bands to meet them, no operas to see, no audiences with high red leaders. For four years as a member of the Communist Party in Russia Smith saw the terrible inequalities, where as he put it: "Every poor peasant who

[23] P. 102

owns nothing is expropriated, where they have taken away his home, his land, his cattle, his products, and his place and left him to starve." [24] Completely disillusioned, Smith returned to America, and the book ends with these words: "We were free at last."

But it is only a waste of time to quote the impartial opinion of those who are not paid propagandists or who have the wool pulled over their eyes by Intourist guides. The conclusion is obvious. Communism has been tried and found wanting. It began as Communism, now admits it has not established it, calls its system Socialism, but in fact it is State Capitalism. Thus it is that the system which begins by hating capitalism takes over all its bad features and ignores its better ones. Communism was right in saying that capitalism ignored the family rights of the worker, but Communism went one better than capitalism, by destroying the family and making the worker the unit of society. Communism was right in saying that capitalism reduced the worker to a "hand," but Communism went one better by ignoring his spiritual qualities altogether, and treating him as a "stomach" to be fed in order to pile up more wealth for the State. Communism was right in saying that capitalism ignored the workers' rights to share, but Communism ignored not only the worker but the peasant by absorbing them both as employees of the State. Capitalism made the ownership of productive private property difficult, but Communism made it impossible. Communism is rotted capitalism. If ever one wants a concrete proof that not even the Communists believe in

[24] P. 290

Communism where it has been tried, just offer to pay their expenses back to the "Paradise." of Russia, in order that they might enjoy its so-called "liberty" and "democracy" for the rest of their lives and see how many will accept. Not even the red leaders in America would go. They prefer to enjoy our liberty in order to destroy it, rather than surrender it, to live in the very slavery their own system has created. They know that the whole world has begun to find them out, namely, that Communism is the greatest system ever devised by the human brain to make the rich poor and the poor miserable, but the worst ever devised to make the poor rich and the workers free.

Chapter IV

Fraternity

How solve the social problem? Liberalism and capitalism answer: "Let every man be free to conduct his business as he pleases." Liberalism and capitalism had their liberty and produced only economic slavery and inequality. Communism then suggested a cure for inequalities: "Confiscate all productive private property in the name of the collectivity and there will be no more classes." Communism had its equality and it destroyed liberty and produced the new inequality of privilege. Now we come to the Catholic solution which says that a reconstruction of the social order must begin not with liberty, nor with equality, but with fraternity.

In order to understand the role of fraternity take a glance at the present order which needs to be remedied. What is its dominant note? Without any hesitation: class struggle between Capital and Labor. "Society today still remains in a strained and therefore uncertain and unstable state, being founded on classes with contradictory interests and hence opposed to each other, and consequently prone to enmity and strife." [1] Capital and Labor consider each other as enemies or a force to be conquered; the force of money and influence, on the one hand, is too often pitted against the force of mass and organization and violence on the other. "The demand and

[1] *Quadragesimo Anno*

51

the supply of labor divides men in the labor market into two classes, or into two camps, and the bargaining between these parties transforms this labor market into an arena where the two armies are engaged in combat. To this pure disorder which is leading society to ruin, a remedy must be evidently applied as speedily as possible." [2]

Communism, instead of diminishing this class hatred, seeks to intensify it so as to disturb the peace of society and prepare for the Communist revolution. "This includes a combination of strikes and armed demonstrations, and finally, the general strike conjointly with armed insurrection against the state power." [3] "The latter form of struggle must be conducted according to the rules of military science; it presupposes a plan of campaign and offensive fighting operations." [4]

The former classes are to be overthrown by a revolution, "bloody and bloodless," violent and peaceful" against the forces and tradition of the old society." [5] Revolution is not only necessary because there is no other way of overthrowing the ruling class, but also because only in the process of revolution is the overthrowing class able to purge itself of the dross of the old society and become capable of creating a new society." [6]

Communism, on its own testimony, does not attempt

[2]*Quadragesimo Anno*
[3]Program, p. 80.
[4]Ibid., p. 81.
[5]Ibid., p. 48.
[6]Ibid., p. 52.

to diminish the class hatred; it rather attempts to develop it, until it can, in its own words, succeed in the "violent overthrow of armies, police, bureaucratic hierarchy and the judiciary." [7] This is a queer way indeed to establish industrial peace. It talks peace but prepares for war; it forbids strikes in Russia but incites them here; it rightly protests against violence directed towards it, and yet insists on the right to use violence on others; it builds a Paradise by first making a wreck of the world; it establishes a classless class by throwing classes at one another's throats; it boasts that it does away with two classes, and yet establishes in its own country about nineteen classes of privilege; it urges all labor unions to a general strike, but yet purges all who would think of it in their fatherland. Its whole system is wrong; you cannot build health in a nation by spreading germs; you cannot educate people by burning the schools; you cannot inaugurate justice by injustice and murder; neither can you do away with classes by intensifying class feeling, nor restore industrial peace by going to war. We will never have social order by inciting Capital and Labor to violence, any more than we will have domestic peace by arming wives with rolling pins to knock all affection out of their husbands' heads. Increase of darkness is not the way to light; brotherhood, equality, and friendship among men can no more come out of envy, hate, violence, purges than honesty can come from giving thieves the privilege of stealing. It is just sheer nonsense to say that the evils of capitalism must get worse and worse before society can

[7]*Ibid., p. 36.*

get better.

Contrast this with the Catholic solution. It starts with the same fact as Communism, namely, the existence of class hatred. Instead of considering Capital and Labor as irreconcilable enemies who must battle until death, it considers them as necessarily related, for in the production of anything three factors cooperate: Capital, Labor, and brains. Instead of overthrowing the present society by revolution and bloodshed, the Catholic solution aims at reconstructing society on the basis of mutual cooperation, joint effort, harmonious organization, justice, charity, and a love of the common good. This, in general, is the meaning of fraternity.

Now for the general principles of the Catholic solution, the details of which must be left to legislation.

Society is presently organized on the basis of rights; the Church should reconstruct it on the basis of function. At present, the word most often used by both Capital and Labor is the word "right." During the past century, capitalism insisted on its "rights" which meant generally the "right to profit." Lately, the pendulum has swung to the other extreme, where Labor is insisting on its "rights," which to extremists means the right to use violence, and the right to all the profits of industry. This reaction was inevitable. Thus it is that today the so-called "rights" of Capital are in conflict with the so called "rights" of Labor, both of which can be equally intolerant, inhuman, and anti-social.

But how many of us have ever heard Capital or Labor use the word "duty"? How often has Capital or Labor used the words "our responsibility"? How often have both used the words "our mutual obligation"? It is the position of the Church that economic peace can reign only when these words begin to have meaning to the warring parties. The Church says that you cannot have any rights without corresponding duties. Rights and duties are correlative like the concave and convex sides of a saucer. I have a right to life, but I have inseparably the duty to respect the life of others. Since there are no rights without duties then rights and duties have a social character. That is why in Christianity, the highest expression of personality is not in the egoistic assertion of rights but in the service of our fellowmen. Politically and economically this implies that the "right" gives way to "role" or "function." This is the Church's solution: Reconstruct society not on selfish "rights" but on the basis of *function*, for "men must be bound together not according to the position they occupy in the labor market" (i.e., not by their income) "but according to the diverse *functions* which they exercise in society." [8]

The difference between a society founded on rights and founded on function is basic. Rights, in the modern sense, are individual; functions are social in the sense that they look to the good of all, and yet both are inseparable, for many rights depend on functions. For example, my eye has a *right* to see, but it cannot exercise that right except by recognizing its *duty* to remain part of the body. So long as the eye *functions* in the organism, it enjoys its rights.

[8]*Quadragesimo Anno*

My heart has the right to blood, but it cannot exercise that function unless it so loves the common good of the organism as to fulfill its duty of sending blood through all the other members of the human body. What is true of the human order *physically* is true of the social order *vocationally*. Capital and Labor, from this point of view, are related and made inseparable from the common good of society. This is the foundation of *social* justice.

Social justice is not to be identified with hating the capitalists or hating the labor racketeers, any more than it is to be identified with the selfish rights of either. This is what both capitalism and Communism forget. The right of the capitalist to his capital, and the right of the laborer to his union, are both conditioned upon the serv. ices they render to society; they both require social justification and hence are both conditioned by their service to the common good, just as the right to drive an automobile can be revoked if one refuses to respect the lives of pedestrians.

This solution of the Church is radical because it avoids the two extremes of capitalism and Communism, and often for that reason, comes in between the fires of both. Capitalism, in the extreme sense of the term, opposes the Church, not because its program lessens the opportunity for industrial peace, but because it lessens the opportunity for capitalist profit; not because it would impoverish the country, but because it will not enrich the capitalists themselves. Communism, on the other hand, opposes it, not because it establishes the reign of social justice, but because it does not establish the dictatorship of the red leaders; not because it makes Capital and Labor live in harmony, but because it does not make them live in hate. In the eyes of the Church, the right to profit on the part of Capital, and the right to organize on the part of Labor, are not *primary*, but secondary. What is primary is that both function for the good of all concerned, so that to no one class but to all will descend social advantages or, in the language of the Encyclical, that "all and each can secure those goods which the wealth and resources of nature, technical achievements and the social organization of economic affairs make possible." [9]

In order to secure this common good in which individuals are more conscious of their functions than their rights, the Church suggests not violence but "social legislation." It goes further and states that "social legislation should aim at the establishment of vocational groups," [10] i.e., groups which have different "functions or occupations or vocations in society." Up until now, society has been organized on the basis of two groups: Capital and Labor: or "two camps (Capital and Labor), and the bargaining between these two parties transforms the labor market into an arena where the two armies are engaged in combat. To this grave disorder which is leading society to ruin, a remedy must be applied as speedily as possible. But there cannot be question of any perfect cure, except the opposition is done away with and well ordered

[9]Ibid.
[10]Ibid.

members of the social body come into being anew, i.e., vocational groups, binding men together not according to the position they occupy in the labor market, but according to the *diverse* functions they exercise in society." [11]

In order to understand what the Church means by a functional society, one may invoke the analogy of the human body. The human body could not function if it were all eyes or all ears. Order is dependent on diverse organs and members working together for the benefit of the whole organism. "Just as in a living organism, it is impossible to provide for the good of the whole unless each single part and each single member is given what it needs for the exercise of its proper function, so it is impossible to care for the social organism and the good of society as a whole, unless each single part and each individual member is supplied with all that is necessary for the exercise of his social function." [12]

Just as the body is not made up of only body and head, so neither is society made up of only Capital and Labor. The body has many organs, e.g., heart, lungs, eyes, etc., and each organ has a different function, e.g., the heart to circulate blood; the lungs to breathe; the eye to see, etc., and all cooperate for the good of the whole. In like manner, just as in the human body the various organs do not live by class hatred, and as the eye does not hate the ear because it hears, nor does the hand hate the foot because it walks, but as all live in harmony by fulfilling

[11]Ibid.
[12]Ibid.

their respective functions, so too will society find its peace by uniting its various groups and occupations for the common good. But there is this difference between the human organism and the social organism: an eye can never become an ear, nor the hand a foot, but in the social order a carpenter may become a farmer, and the ditch digger a banker. In order to reveal this free activity of an individual within society as different to the enforced activity of a cell within the body, the Church uses the term "vocational," i.e., the individual's social performance may be likened to a vocation.

Instead then, of organizing society into two camps of Capital and Labor as two enemies with a grudge, society will be organized on the basis of function into various groups or guilds varying in nature and number with the contribution each group makes to society as a whole, i.e., "those who practice the same trade or profession combine into vocational groups." [13] "Just as citizens within the same city are wont to form associations with diverse aims, [e.g., athletic, political, social, religious, economic,] which various individuals are free to join or not, similarly those who are engaged in the same trade or profession, [e.g., lawyers, farmers, clerical workers, engineers, etc.,) will form free associations among themselves, for purposes connected with their occupations." Instead then of society being divided into two warring classes, Capital and Labor, it will be composed of various groups, or guilds, or corporations varying in number with the role they play in

[13] Ibid.

in society. This is a normal order, for just as men who live together form a town" so those who work together (practice the same profession") should form an occupational group. [14] For example, let there be a vocational or occupational group composed of miners, farmers, textile workers, auto-workers, civil service workers, railroad, telegraph and telephone men, carpenters, doctors, lawyers, steelworkers, etc., and perhaps twenty or thirty other groups depending upon their function in society. Under such an arrangement society is divided not into classes but into professions.

These groups or guilds include not only organized employees but also organized employers in each professional group. The reason for this is that there is a common interest between members of the same trade or profession. Professional and trade groups organize not to show their power or violence against one another, not to intimidate either, but to settle their corporate differences by peaceful means. The representatives of the employers and the representatives of the employees in any given group, e.g., the legal group, the textile group, should then form joint boards, meeting in regular sessions for the discussion of all disagreements as well as the promotion of their mutual interests. Or, to use the words of the Encyclical: "It is most opportune, useful and in conformity with Christian principles to continue, as far as may be practicable, the simultaneous establishment of separate unions for employers and for workers, while creating, as a

[14]Ibid.

point of contact between them, joint committees, entrusted with the duty of discussing and settling, in a peaceful manner, in accordance with justice and charity, the disagreements that may spring up between the members of the respective unions." [15] By such an arrangement classes based on income and wealth would be done away with, and the concept of professions would dominate society. The worker would be elevated from the rank of a passive recipient of salary to that of an effective collaborator endowed with a sense of personal responsibility and dignity.

A society which is divided into Capital and Labor has no real internal unity. The Church's solution gives Labor "a unity of common profession, the unity of a common effort of employers and employees of one and the same group joining forces to produce goods or give service, and the unity of the common good which all groups should unite to promote, each in its own sphere with friendly harmony." [16]

The Church furthermore suggests that since modern industrial life is extremely complex and one group is dependent upon another group, as the automobile industry is dependent on the steel industry, there be an interrelation between the various occupational groups. Just as the hand in the human body has one function or profession, and the foot has another function or profession, but all unite for the orderly working of the whole organism, so too the textile group, the auto group,

[15]Ibid.
[16]Ibid.

the farmer group, the banking group, each made up of employers and employees, would work together, and direct all their forces and endeavors for a higher task, namely, the good of the whole nation and the betterment of humanity. This would imply the federation of all the groups through representatives into a national council which would be the intermediary between the individual and the State.

A final and most important point is the role the State plays in relation to the professional groups. The position of the Church is clear: it avoids two erroneous extremes: the extreme in which the State has nothing to say, which is individualism, and the extreme in which the State has everything to say, which is Fascism and Communism. For the functioning of these groups, it is important that the State have more to say than it did under liberalism, and less to say than it does under Fascism or Communism. For liberalism the State was a policeman, never daring to interfere with business under penalty of violating its so-called "liberty." For Communism and Fascism, the State is a nurse, taking care of individuals and groups from the cradle to the grave and depriving them of their just autonomy. In between these two extremes of the State being *indifferent* to business, and the State *controlling and managing* business or making it "serve particular political aims," [17] as is the case under Nazism and Fascism, is the golden mean of the State "contributing to the initiation of a better social order. . . . The State would watch over these

[17]Ibid.

societies of citizens united together in the exercises of their rights; but the State must not thrust itself into their *particular* concerns and their organization for things move and live by the souls within while they may be killed by the grasp of the soul without." [18]

Let it be repeated that this solution of the Church implies a distinction between politics and economics, i.e., between the State and these professional groups. It repudiates the Fascist, the Nazi, and the Communist solutions because all three give the State supreme authority over these unions of Capital and Labor and hence destroy their freedom and autonomy. Because the Church insists that the form these corporations or associations take be left to themselves, it follows that such associations would not involve any change in the structure of our government. The guild order has no identification with any kind of political order. It will fit into any system and would particularly fit into our own. It will fit perfectly if we avoid the pitfalls of Fascism, Nazism, and Communism in which the groups and unions are subservient to the State or a party. In the Catholic view, the State is the servant of the groups, not the groups the tool of the State. The Catholic solution avoids the Communist and Fascist evils of putting the majority at the mercy of a dictatorial minority and the other extreme of a capitalism which puts the majority at the mercy of the minority of greedy economic exploiters.

[18]Ibid.

In brief, the Church's position is this: "the reign of mutual collaboration between justice and charity in social-economic relations can only be achieved by a body of professional and inter-professional organizations, built on solidly Christian foundations, working together to effect, under forms adapted to different places and circumstances, the common good." [19]

This is one of the basic concrete proposals of the Church for social peace, and there is no just man who will deny that its charity and justice is a better method of reform than the violence of Communism. Just dwell for a moment on one line in the Communist Program, namely, "ruthless suppression of resistance." Now let us ask ourselves the question: "What kind of a social order, other than the disorder of Russia, can be built by 'ruthlessly suppressing'" all who do not believe in the violence of Communism?" To remedy conflict of classes by the suppression of a class is like settling a domestic quarrel by killing the husband. Violence bent on destruction is no good for construction. The carpenter who gets more fun out of breaking windows than by putting them in, cannot build the kind of house you and I would want to live in.

We are not meant to hate one another, for we are all one because citizens of a country which has been blessed by the Creator with more natural wealth than any country on the face of the globe; we are all one too, because members of a common humanity, who can recite a common prayer to a common Father, "Our Father, Who

[19] *Divini Redemptoris.*

art in Heaven"; we are all one, too, at least, potentially, because we are all called to be united in the supernatural society, where, by eating one Bread, we become one Body in the Lord. Justice and charity, not hate and violence, is the only guiding spirit of lives. The universalism for which the Church strives is not that of a class, but of humanity; it unites men, not because they hate capitalism, but because they love justice; not because they are anti-Fascist or anti-Communist or anti-anything, but because they are *Pro-Deo, pro-bono publico*. It respects men and women in our nation, not because they glory in Russia with its purges, but because they glory in America with its freedom.

Justice and charity -- upon these virtues rather than upon great wealth or great power is the strength of a nation built. Justice there must be to temper the excesses of a false liberty which allows a man to amass wealth without social responsibilities; charity there must be to mitigate the class hatred which Communism would enflame. But justice and charity there cannot be without a firm belief in the God Who judges and the God Who forgives. Upon the recognition of that God our nation was founded and only under that common Father can we call one another brother." Only when we recognize the God from Whom every grace and blessing comes, can we understand the symbol of our democracy. It is not a hammer and a sickle, a swastika, or a bundle of sticks, all of which smack of the earth earthy. It is a bird -- not an owl that hoots in darkness, nor a bat that haunts blackness; not a sparrow that stays close to the earth, nor a vulture that thinks only of prey. Rather, with a full consciousness that our rights and our freedom come from beyond the highest mountain and the most distant star, did America, in the language of Chesterton, choose the eagle whose "glory is gazing at the sun."

Chapter V

Distribution

From the idea of fraternity, flows distribution. We begin with the fact which Communists, Socialists, Fascists, Jews, Protestants, and Catholics have in common; viz., the unequal distribution of wealth, its concentration in the hands of the few, and the impoverishment of the masses. There are only three possible ways to remedy this inequality: Firstly, continue capitalism, in which the man who has nothing must work for the man who has everything; in which the worker is politically free, but economically enslaved; in which the problems of justice are settled by a display of force and a civil war, with strikes as the weapon of one army and injunctions the weapon of the other. Or secondly, accept Communism, which cures the evil of unequal distribution of wealth by violently confiscating all productive private property, overthrowing the government, and establishing in its place a dictatorship over the proletariat, such as exists in Russia. Or thirdly, distribution of productive private property, which is the Catholic solution. More simply: Capitalism stands for possession through individual selfishness. Communism stands for dispossession through collective selfishness; the Church stands for distribution through charity and justice. The first solution or the continuation of capitalism will not do, for it has already proven its inadequacy. The second solution, or Communism, will not do, for making all men work for a few red commissars has no advantage over making them work for a few capitalists. Apart too, from the disruption of society by violence and revolution, the break with tradition, the surrender of liberty to a dictator, Communism forgets that, as Aristotle said centuries ago, that "which is the business of everyone is the business of no one." Under Communism, the factory belongs to the workers, in the same way, the public parks belong to us. And yet how many Americans do you see going into the parks to pick up refuse on Monday morning, or mending a hole in the pavement? When you get a few bureaucrats deciding how many pairs of trousers have to be made for the workers, you very soon reach a condition described by the Commissar of the food industry in Russia, Mikoyan, "We are accustomed in the Soviet Republic to have only goods of bad quality and always in insufficient quantities."[1] Freedom leaves where everything is planned, even the food you eat. Anyone with ideas of his own is just as much a nuisance to planned economy as to an army at war. When the dictatorship of the proletariat is set up, to whom do the proletariat dictate? And what happens if a worker holds an opinion contrary to the dictator? The answer is he is "liquidated" or "purged" or sometimes just "disappears." To dictate to a dictator is the shortest cut to a tombstone.

[1] Statement made at the Plenary Session of the Central Committee of the C. P. December, 1935. *Investia*, December 27, 1935.

Contrary to Communist propaganda which tells us that the world must choose between capitalism and Communism, the Church insists there is a third choice and a golden mean, namely, distribution, or the wider diffusion of private property, both productive and consumptive.

There are two steps by which the Church proposes to secure greater economic freedom for the worker by distribution. 1. The payment of a living wage. 2. Securing for the worker, when possible, a share in the "ownership, profits and management" of the industry in which he works.

I. "The wage contract is not essentially unjust," [2] but it may be accidentally unjust by refusing to pay a living wage. "Social justice cannot be said to have been satisfied as long as workingmen are denied a salary that will enable them to secure proper sustenance for them. selves and for their families, as long as they are denied the opportunity of acquiring a modest fortune and forestalling the plague of universal pauperism; as long as they cannot make suitable provision through a public or private insurance for old age, for periods of illness and unemployment." [3] "Then only will the economic and social order be soundly established and attain its ends, when it offers to all and to each, all those goods which the wealth and resources of nature, technical science and the corporate organization of social affairs can give. These goods should be sufficient to supply all

[2] *Ouadragesimo Anno.*
[3] *Divini Redemptoris.*

necessities and reasonable comforts and to uplift men to that higher standard of life which, provided it be used with prudence, is not a hindrance but is of singular help to virtue."[4]

How far are we from a living wage in the United States! For 1936 average weekly earnings in the manufacturing industries were $22.36; in cotton $13.55; in laundries $16.04; in automobiles $28.78; in hotels $13.96. It is the contention of the Church that most of these wages are insufficient. But if the employers refuse to pay the wages, may the State by legislation give special consideration to the poor? The answer is in the affirmative. "The rich population have many ways of protecting themselves, and stand less in need of help from the State; those who are badly off have no resources of their own to fall back upon, and must chiefly rely upon the assistance of the State. And it is for this reason, that wage earners, who are undoubtedly among the weak and necessitous, should be specially cared for and protected by the State."[5]

In the concrete, the Church asserts that the wages of the worker must not merely be sufficient for the necessities of life, but should enable the worker to "possess" a certain modest fortune; that "bad management, want of enterprise, or out of date methods is not a just reason for reducing the workingmen's wages," [6] that the right of the worker to a living wage comes before the employer's right to enlarge his plant or the

[4]*Quadragesimo Anno* and *Divini Redemptoris.*
[5]*Reraum Novarum.*
[6]*Quadragesimo Anno.*

employer's right to advertise to increase his sales. The human factor in industry comes before the economic factor. Buying new office furniture to escape a higher income tax when the stenographers are receiving only $15 a week is wrong and can never be justified as long as a human being is worth more than the chair on which he sits or the desk at which he works.

How many employers are there in the United States who can say there is not a single employee who is receiving less than $100 a month or its equivalent? How many Catholic employers are doing so? Let all who are paying a living wage (and $100 a month is not a living family wage) advertise that fact; let them boast not of the high quality of their products, nor the great quantity of their output, but their faithful discharge of human obligations, and we will have the beginning of a true social order that will mock a regime such as exists in Russia where the average worker has to labor nearly a month to earn enough to buy a pair of shoes.

In asserting that the worker shall have a living wage which should be "sufficient to keep himself and family in reasonable and frugal comfort"[7] the Church avoids two extreme errors: 1. the error of capitalism "claiming all the products and profits" for the employers; and 2. the error of Marxism claiming that all products and profits, excepting those required to repair and replace invested

[7]*Rerum Novarum.*

capital belong by every right to the working man." [8] In the golden mean is the principle of just distribution which "forbids one class to exclude the other from a share in the profits."

II. The Church looks beyond even the payment of a living wage. Here we hit upon the very essence of the Catholic solution. "In the present state of human society we deem it advisable that the wage contract should, when possible, be modified by a contract of partnership. ... In this way wage-earners are made sharers in some way, in the ownership, or the management, or the profits" of industry. [9]

The argument the Church urges for a modification of the wage system by giving the proletariat some capital, reveals a principle which the modern world has completely forgotten, namely, that hired labor has an "individual and social aspect." [10] It has an *individual* character because personally performed through moral duty or necessity. Labor has also a *social* character. This is particularly evident when a man hires himself out to labor for another. The social character of his labor is there revealed by the fact that he is part of an order in which "brains, capital, and labor combine for common fruit." [11] Furthermore, the succession of his laboring days, the raising of a family for society, the education of children for the next generation, all constitute a social contribution.

[8]*Quadragesimo Anno*
[9]Ibid.
[10]Ibid.
[11]Ibid.

Now what returns does the worker receive for his labor? For his individual contribution, the worker receives wages, with their twin fears of unemployment and insecurity. But what does he receive for his social contributions, his constantly deteriorating physical strength, and his constantly increasing contribution to the common good? Presently, except in a few instances, he receives nothing. Wages recompense him for his hours by the clock, but they do not recompense him for the new wealth that is created in cooperation with "brains and capital." That is where the suggestion of the Holy Father comes in the worker should be entitled to some share in the "ownership or management or the profits" of industry. In other words, since he makes a social contribution he should also receive a social reward. Capitalism says the capitalist may "claim all the profits"[12] while the worker has a right only to his wages, which are often insufficient. Communism, going to the opposite extreme, says that the worker has the right to the whole product" which would be an injustice to the one who owned capital. "Such men, vehemently incensed against the violation of justice by the capitalists go too far in vindicating the one right of which they are conscious." [13] The Church says: "*Neither class must be excluded from a share in the profits.*" Wealth must be so distributed among the various individuals and classes of society that the common good of all be promoted ... "for the vast difference between the few who hold excessive wealth and the many who live in destitution constitutes a grave

[12]Ibid.
[13]Ibid.

evil in modern society." [14]

The next question is how and why should it be done? How will this be done? By violence? No! By confiscation? No! By educating the employer? Yes. By law? Yes! "The law should favor ownership and its policy should be to induce as many as possible to become owners." This is a call not to give workers only personal consumptible property or a bonus, but even productive property.

Why should it be done? Because from a wider distribution of property three benefits would follow:

a. It would diminish class hatred and the "gulf between vast wealth and deep poverty will be bridged over and the two classes will be brought closer together. [15]

b. "There will be greater abundance of the fruits of the earth. Men always work harder and more readily when they work on that which is their own ... and would therefore add to the wealth of the community." [16]

c. It would make people more patriotic for "men would cling to the country in which they were born; for no one would exchange his country for a foreign land if his own afforded him the means of living a tolerable and happy life." [17]

For the Catholic then, the defense of the present system of capitalism in which wealth is in the hands of a

---

[14] Ibid.
[15] *Rerum Novarum.*
[16] Ibid.
[17] Ibid.

few is almost as wrong as the Communist solution which would destroy that wealth and appropriate it all in the hands of the red leaders. The Communists want to "break up" capitalism, by making the State capitalistic and the workers proletarians or wage earners; the Church wants to "break down" capitalism by making the workers share "in the profits, management or ownership" of industry. The Communists want to concentrate, the Church wants to distribute. The society in which there are as many owners as possible is not something which we Catholics may only discuss; it is something we must propagate and institute. The Church is just as much opposed as Communism to the propertyless wage earner, but it proposes to remedy the situation, not by giving all the productive property to the dictator, but by giving some of it to the workers themselves. The violent abolition of productive private property, which Communism advocates and the restriction of productive private property to a few men which capitalism fosters are both to be condemned in favor of as wide a distribution of property as possible. Since every business is constituted not only of money-capital but also of labor-capital, it is unfair that all the control and profits should be left to the former.

The Church does not believe in putting all the eggs in one basket, but in giving a man a right to own a few eggs, especially if he wants to raise chickens and thus become a capitalist himself, in the sense that property is the economic guarantee of his freedom. By distributing a wide mass of property owners throughout the country with their scattered powers, privileges, and responsibilities, one creates the greatest resistance in the world to tyranny, either political or economic, and also to foreign propaganda, either Fascist or Communist. Man likes liberty, likes to extend his personality by ownership, likes to call things his own, likes certain kinds of local affection, and these things the Church proposes to give him.

One day in a discussion with a Communist I argued: "Do you not believe, my friend, that instead of talking always about wages, we should rather seek to peacefully distribute productive capital, by giving to the worker the external sign of his internal freedom and responsibility, namely, property?" To which he retorted: "That was all right in the Middle Ages, but remember we live in a complex civilization. How distribute the spoils, e.g., of the United States Steel Corporation?" To this was given the answer: "If you find it difficult to divide the spoils of the United States Steel Corporation, how in heaven's name do you expect to distribute the spoils of all the corporations, banks and factories of the United States after you confiscate them during a revolution?" His only reaction was: "Let's change the subject."

But that is just the subject we refuse to change. When the Church holds for a worker sharing in the wealth he produces, it does not propose mathematically equal distribution, but a sufficient distribution to give a tone and a spirit to society. Neither does the Church mean a return to small craftsmanship, for ownership of small things and distribution of ownership are not identical.

At the present time, many a worker is not economically free because he lacks a possession to which he can give the imprint of his own will. To have his life ordered by others, who have no other authority than that they own the place where he works, is not freedom. That is why capitalism will not do. Neither will a mere sharing the wealth in the hands of the State do, for what is the use of sharing the wealth unless you have something to say about it? It is not shared wealth workers want, for workers who receive wealth because the State sees that they do, are slaves. If the State withdraws its patronage, they are left with nothing. There is very little difference between a worker losing his job because a capitalist discharges him or because a Communist liquidates him. Self-government and responsibility, which are the attributes of freedom, are impossible when the capitalists own all or when the red leaders own all.

In between these two extremes of capitalism and Communism is a reconstructed order which secures the political and economic freedom of the worker. To the great credit of some modern industrialists, these pleas of Leo XIII and Pius XI are already being put into practice, and the workers are being given some share in the profits they helped to create. The president of one corporation -- Harmon P. Elliot of the Addressing Machine Co. -- set up an irrevocable trust fund of $250,000 (one half of his personal fortune) invested in 7 percent cumulative stock of his company, the returns of which are to be paid to his workers, and this after increasing the salaries of 350 workers $85,000 a year. Another industrialist -- George

R. Rich of the G. R. Rich Mfg. Co. -- offered $1,500 worth of stock to each of his employees and gave them the right to elect three directors to the corporation's board of eight, and assured them that first dividends would be paid to employee stockholders. Another large corporation -- Eastman Kodak Co -- authorized, in the first quarter of the year, a dividend to the employees, which was almost twice the amount given to the stockholders. An even larger corporation -- Endicott Johnson Shoe Co. -- has so much taken to heart the suggestion of Leo XIII that it gives to every worker, share for share, on the basis of seniority and merit, every dollar the business earns over costs and dividends to stockholders. In addition to this, there is free hospitalization, medical care, and recreational activities. Another corporation -- Jantzen Knitting Mills of Portland, Oregon announces the same plan for the workers, thus giving them a share in the profits of the company in proportion to their annual wage, and in many cases, this amounts to a $500,000 increase over the annual wage. [18] Another firm -- Joslyn Mfg. & Supply Co. of Chicago permits the employee to invest 5 percent of his earnings with the company. The company, in its turn, pays four times that amount into a fund controlled by a trustee, which becomes available to the worker at the age of sixty. If he leaves earlier, he receives three-fifths of the total. The fund in the course of the last 19 years has earned an average of 9 percent compounded. Under this

---

[18] Dr. Joseph F. Thorning has presented these and many other facts in a brilliant article in the Commonweal, July 16, 1937.

arrangement an employee who has paid into the fund $100 a year for 18 years, which is $1,800, now has a credit of $16,500. The president of this corporation said of his plan: "It has given us men unafraid of dependency or old age, men with a steadily growing stake in the country and its institutions -- defenders of capital because they have capital to defend."

It was this plan of the Holy Father that one of the great industrialists of the country hoped would find universal application. "I hope," he said, "that the day may come when these great business organizations will truly belong to the men who are giving their lives and their efforts to them. I care not in what capacity. Then they will use capital truly as a tool and they will be all interested in working it to the highest advantage. Then an idle machine will mean to every man in the plant who sees it an unproductive charge against himself. Then we shall have zest in labor, provided the leadership is competent and the division fair. Then we shall dispose once and for all of the charge that in industry organizations are autocratic and not democratic. Then we shall have all the opportunities for a cultural wage which the business can provide. Then, in a word, men will be as free in cooperative undertakings and subject only to the same limitations and chances as men in individual business." [19]

There is a golden mean between selfishness and dispossession, and that is sharing and distribution. Such is the Catholic solution, and it is one which will demand

[19]. Owen D. Young

sacrifices which, up to the present, the majority of capitalists have been unprepared to make. Either big business in this country will share its profits with the workers as the Church asks, or it will be in danger of having its business confiscated by violent hands. There is no middle course. Either they will give freely, or they will surrender involuntarily. Why should the employers monopolize for themselves tremendous reserves for depreciation and give themselves vast bonuses, and yet make little or no provision for the social contribution of the employees who helped to create that wealth? "Social justice cannot be said to have been satisfied as long as workingmen are denied the opportunity of acquiring a modest fortune and forestalling the plagues of universal pauperism, as long as they cannot make suitable provision through public and private insurance for old age, for perils of illness and employment." [20]

The Church is not opposed to Communism only because it is anti-religious and anti-God, or because it is violent, revolutionary, and disruptive of culture. The Church is opposed to Communism also because it enslaves the worker by keeping his body and soul chained to a dictator: his body chained because the dictator has all the jobs; his soul chained because he must think what the dictator thinks. Furthermore, the Church believes that one of the greatest obstacles in the way of effectively combating the evils of Communism is "the foolhardiness of those who neglect to remove or modify unjust conditions which are exasperating the minds of the people and

[20] *Divini Redemptoris.*

preparing the way for the overthrow and ruin of the social order." Remove the environment in which Communism grows, and you do much to remove the menace of Communism -- not remove it completely of course, for it would not be satisfied with a Paradise, if there were no dictatorship over the proletariat and the enforced irreligion of the masses. But if our great industrialists would sit down with their heads between their hands, read over these encyclicals of the Holy Father, and then announce their dividends not only on the financial pages of our newspapers but also on the bulletin boards of their factories; if they made their laborers "sharers in ownership, profit or management," as the Encyclical asks, then they would need to worry less about the reds. And the Communists know this, they admit that it is difficult for Communism to grow where business conditions are just. As their own official International Press Correspondent states: "The radicalization of the workers and their increasing impoverishment is the best soil for Communism." [21] That means Communists want to see the workers kept in a lowly and unjust condition, for then they can incite them to violence. But share the wealth with the workers, help them to become owners and sharers in the industry or factory or business where they work, and they will think twice before they will follow the Communist cry for violence. They will see that they would not be destroying your property alone but *theirs* also. They will sit down on your machines, but they will not sit down on

[21] August 10, 1935

their own. Then the Communists will no longer be able to incite hatred against capitalists, for the workers will be capitalists themselves, i.e., owners of the productive capital which the Communists would seize. Then we will have an industrial order in which 20,000 men will not say, for example: "I am working for such and such a corporation, but "we are working *with* them." Then when their agitators come to your plants to incite violence, your co-partners, the workers, will do what they did last year to the president of one of the corporations which shared dividends and management with them, namely, refuse to follow the inciters of violence. They even went further and addressed the president of the corporation -- George F. Johnson of the Endicott Johnson Shoe Co. -- as follows: "At this time when industrial strife is rampant through the nation, when capital and labor are in the throes of suspicion and distrust with each other, each hurling open accusations at the other and attempting to impair the security of industry by their efforts to dominate, we want to stand fast by that old proverb: "Hold fast to that which is good."

There is no labor trouble in an industry where there is no Labor in the sense of a group opposed to Capital; there are only partners. Therein is another great and basic difference between the Communistic and the Christian solution. Communism has as its ideal to make everyone a worker -- in the sense that each one works for the dictator who controls the wealth and who is the only employer. Christianity has as its ideal to make everyone a capitalist

-- in the sense that each one owns productive as well as consumptive capital as his own and has the freedom and security which goes with it.

A true social order can be built only on the basis of fraternity; namely, one inspired not by profit motive, which is capitalism; not by the political motive which is Fascism; not by the violence motive which is Communism, but by the love motive which is Christianity. Start with fraternity, which means that all men are brothers under the Fatherhood of God, that all must function for the common good of society and for the peace of the world, and liberty and equality will follow. Liberty will follow, for the masses will then be free from economic want which will leave their souls free to seek that higher destiny to which they are called as heirs of the glorious liberty of the children of God. Equality will follow, for all men will be equal in the possession of inalienable and sacred rights of human personality which no dictator can take away, equal also in their right to share the common heritages of civilization. Gone then will be that false equality of Communism which will tolerate no hierarchy, for equality implies multiplicity in unity; gone will be that false liberty of liberalism which is another name for selfishness. In its place will come the equality which admits of differences and the organic relations of part to part for the proper functioning of the whole and the real freedom which will be powerful enough to enforce freedom. Establish a society of that kind on the basis not of hate but of Charity. Capital and Labor will no longer be at one another's throats. They will meet as partners in the production of social wealth, as citizens of a great republic, and they will salute one another on the streets not by the autonomic name of "Comrade" but by the Christian name of "Brother."

Chapter VI

The Trojan Horse

The Holy Father, in his letter on Atheistic Communism, sounds this warning note concerning the tactics of Communism: "In the beginning, Communism showed itself for what it was in all its perversity; but very soon found it was alienating the people. It has therefore changed its tactics, and strives to entice the multitudes by trickery of various forms, hiding its real designs behind ideas that are in themselves good and attractive. ... They carry their hypocrisy so far as to encourage the belief that Communism, in countries where faith and culture are more strongly entrenched, will assume another and much milder form. It will not interfere with the practice of religion. It will respect liberty of conscience. ... See to it, Venerable Brethren, that the faithful do not allow themselves to be deceived! Communism is intrinsically wrong, and no one may collaborate with it in any undertaking whatsoever. Those who permit themselves to be deceived into lending their aid towards the triumph of Communism in their own country will be the first to fall victims of their error."

This indictment of Communism is not too severe, for everything the Holy Father says about Communistic methods, Communism itself admits. In order to prove this point, one need only consult Communist sources.

The point to be proven is this: Communism has changed its tactics, but not its end or purpose, namely, the revolutionary overthrow of the existing order.

When Communism began in Russia in 1917 it was generally expected that within a few years the whole of Europe would be in the throes of a Communistic revolution. For that reason, Moscow instructed its delegates in various parts of the world to openly preach revolution and practice violence. The world quickly seeing that Paradises are not built by bloodshed reacted against the violence of Communism and defeated it. The dictatorship of Bela Kun collapsed in Hungary: the Poles arose *en masse* when the destructive Communists marched on Warsaw; Hitler arose in Germany and Mussolini in Italy under the threat of a Communist menace. In other words, Communism finally saw in its own words that "it could not exercise such direct influences upon the working class as Russian Bolshevism exercised upon the fresh, revolutionary material it had to deal with, which had not yet become saturated with reformist influences. The spontaneous element plays a less important role in the mass movement in modern countries than it did in pre-revolutionary Russia."[1]

Another reason for the failure of Communism to achieve its revolutionary end by preaching revolution was the fewness of Communists. As the official spokesman of Communism has put it: "In the overwhelming majority of capitalist countries, the Communists are too weak to lead the masses directly into the fight for the establishment of

[1]D. Z Manuilsky, *The Work of the Seventh Congress*, P. 59 and 60.

the proletarian dictatorship." [2] Hence the necessity of changing the approach in order to effect the revolution. Accordingly, in July and August of 1935, it called the Seventh World Congress of Communism which decided to change the tactics of Communism. From that point on it resolved to use non-revolutionary language in the open to attain revolutionary ends in secret.

Without openly admitting that the world would not have a revolution simply because Russia had one, the Seventh World Congress now decides its former tactics were wrong. The world was not yet ready for revolution, conditions were not the same elsewhere as in Europe, and the majority of mankind still believes the best way to heal social ills is by legislation and not by revolution.

To accommodate themselves to the modern mentality, the Communists decided to cease talking revolution and to begin talking "democracy," "peace" and "hatred of Fascism," "jobs" and "security." Their new program called for a "United Front" or a "Democratic Front" with all groups, parties, or programs on the broadest possible basis of unity. The new method was very much like that of the card shark on a boat who makes friends with his victim on the "united front" grounds that they both love a drink.

The innocent victim does not yet know what the card shark intends to do, but the card shark knows. The affability and the willingness to pay for the drinks, the

[2]Ibid., p. 62.

sleek geniality are all details of his "front" and part of his tactics.

The United Front of Communism is in like manner the false face of Communism. During its existence Communism says nothing about the destruction of private property, nothing about its hatred of religion, nothing about Lenin's statement that Communist dictatorship "rests on violence, limited by no laws or rules." On the contrary, it speaks of its love of America, the rights of the worker, its sympathy for religion, and its passion for democracy.

Does this mean Communism has changed its philosophy, or that it has given up its intention to overthrow the existing order? No! it only means it has decided not to talk about those things *yet*. It is not yet time for the kill. It has merely changed its tactics, but not its principles. To put it all very simply, the United Front is only the technique for the moment, like the card shark's purchase of the drinks. That this is the plain truth we know from Earl Browder, the Executive Secretary of the Communist Party in the United States, who writes in his book, *What is Communism?* "We must emphasize that this United Front government would be a transitional form ... for the masses are not yet prepared to fight for Soviet Power."

In the Gospel language, this means the Democratic Front is the wolf in the clothing of the sheep. These words are nothing else but the echo of the Official Program of the Third International which dictates the methods for what it calls a pre-revolutionary period.

As the Official Program puts it: "Throughout the entire *pro-revolutionary period* a most important basic part of the tactics of the Communist Party is the tactics of the United Front, as a means towards the successful struggle against capital, towards the class mobilization of the masses and the exposure and isolation of the reformist leaders."[3] "Where there is no revolutionary upsurge, the Communist Parties must advance partial slogans and demands that correspond to everyday needs of the toilers, linking them up with the fundamental tasks of the Communist International" of Moscow.[4] "The Party determines its slogans and methods of struggle in accordance with circumstances with the view to organizing and mobilizing the masses on the broadest possible scale. This is done by carrying on propaganda in favor of increasingly radical transitional slogans and the mass action includes a combination of strikes and demonstrations, ... and finally a general strike conjointly with armed insurrection against the State Power."[5]

Analyze these statements. Communism changes its tactics; it no longer talks revolution, it talks against Fascism; it no longer talks arms, it preaches peace; it no longer talks about overthrowing government, it talks about preserving democracy; it no longer talks about butchering the capitalists, it talks about the rights of the worker. In other words, it has changed its complexion,

[3]P. 82.
[4]Program, p. 81.
[5] Ibid, p. 8o.

but has it changed its face? It changes its tactics, but does it change its desire for revolution? It changes its talk, but does it change its mind? It changes its illegal talk, but does it change its illegal methods? It has merely decided that the best way to achieve revolution is not to talk about it, but to work secretly for it. The termites who eat away the porch do not first call at your front door and inform you of their presence, and tell you they propose to make the roof fall on your head. They know they can accomplish more by the Democratic Front tactics of boring from within. You know they have been at work only when the roof falls upon your head.

Such are the new tactics of Communism. They admit that they are, only instead of using the example of termites to explain their new approach, they use the example of the Trojan Horse. The exact words of George Dimitrov to the assembled delegates of the World Communists at the Moscow Congress, among whom was Earl Browder, the Communist candidate for President in the last election, are these: "Comrades, you remember the ancient tale of the capture of Troy. Troy was inaccessible to the armies attacking her, thanks to her impregnable walls. And the attacking army after suffering great losses, was still unable to achieve victory until with the aid of the famous Trojan horse it managed to penetrate to the very heart of the enemy camp." [6] In that large wooden horse were hidden soldiers, which the defenders of Troy never suspected of being in the inside until they arose to seize power.

[6]*Ibid., p. 57*

In like manner Communism is urged to wheel its Trojan horses into our labor unions, religious organizations, political parties, athletic associations, under the guise of a peaceful United Front until it can tear off its mask and turn the country over to a barbarous civil war such as they instigated in Spain, so that it may emerge victorious and thus honor their beloved Comrade Stalin. Their United and Popular Fronts call for a union of Communists with other political organizations, but what these political organizations forget is that Communism uses them only to further its revolutionary ends. Political parties who use the Communists should know the Official Resolution of the Communist International of August 20, 1935. "The unification of social-democratic parties, in any particular organization with the Communist Party, should be subject to the recognition of the *necessity of the revolutionary overthrow of the existing order*, and the installation of the Dictatorship of the proletariat under the Soviets."[7]

But this is not all. Lest anyone should still believe that their seemingly peaceful tactics mean anything less than revolution, it would be well to hear officially from D. Z. Manuilsky who, summarizing the Congress, states: "Tactics, generally, may change, but the general line of the Communist International ... for proletarian revolution ... remains unchanged."[8] In a preceding page, the same Bolshevik also states that the "Communists must actively

[7]*Pravda*, August 6, 1935.
[8] P. 65.

intervene in the present mass movement, strive to raise it to the revolutionary overthrow of capitalism and the establishment of the proletarian dictatorship."[9] Furthermore, Dimitrov said that Communism had intentionally expunged from the reports as well as from the decisions of the Congress *high-sounding phrases* of the revolutionary projective." But he goes on immediately to warn us that they still believe in revolution. "We did this not because we have any ground for appraising the tempo of revolutionary development less optimistically than before." Then he concludes that by using the new tactics which he advocates, they will be doing everything to "accelerate more than in any other way, the creation of the subjective preconditions necessary for the *victory* of the proletarian revolution." [10]

One of the favorite disguises of the new Communistic tactics is to talk about democracy. This is partly because the word "Communism" has a bad odor because of its failure and blood-purges in Russia, and partly because it wishes to win over democratic governments such as France, England, and the United States, and it figures the best way to do this is by using the term "democracy." Communism, of course, is no more interested in furthering the democracy of the United States than Americans are in continuing purges in Russia. When Communism uses the term "democracy" it means Communism. Naturally, some of the old-school Communists felt that in talking

[9]P. 63.
[10] *Op. cit.,* p. 165.

Democracy, Communism had lost its interest in Communism. Dimitrov allays this fear by saying "the circumstance that even today we must still make reference to fear, in our ranks, of launching positive democratic slogans, indicates how little our comrades have mastered the Marxist-Leninist tactics." [11] He even quotes Lenin to prove that when they talk democracy they still intend revolution. "It would be a fundamental mistake to suppose that the struggle for democracy can divert the proletarians from the Socialist revolution or obscure or overshadow it." [12] And Manuilsky says that all who believe that the "united front tactics mean that Communism is capitulating to Social Democracy" are "downright scoundrels and hopeless idiots." [13] And what is all this deceit and hypocrisy but the faithful obedience to the injunction of Lenin to his party? "You must be ready to make all sacrifices, to use all strategy of ruse, all illegal methods; to be quiet when necessary; to conceal the truth in order to penetrate all groups and to incite or do anything to accomplish world revolution." [14]

"The practical duties of Communist policy," Lenin said in his speech of November 16, 1920: "consist of our exploiting the animosity between bourgeois States and inciting the capitalists against each other. The Communists must play each against the other." [15]

[11] P. 128.
[12] P. 129.
[13] Pp. 58, 59.
[14] *The Infantile Malady of Communism.*
[15] Lenin: *Regarding the Treaty of Versailles*, pp. 86, 89.

Now it may be objected that American Communism is not under Moscow, or that the American Communist Party does not believe in Moscow violence and purges. The American Communist Party itself has given the answer to this.

a) Earl Browder, the Executive Secretary of the Communist Party in the United States, testified before the 74th Congress of the United States that the American Communist Party was "a section of the Third International of Moscow and was in contact with it."

b) The Executive Secretary of the Communist Party in the United States is a member of the Plenum of the Third International of Moscow which controls Communistic propaganda and activity throughout the world.

c) The Executive Secretary of the Communist Party in the United States on July 27, 1935, gave a 90-minute report on Communistic activities in the United States to the Executive Secretary of the Communist International and delegates in Moscow and acted as the chairman of the 7th session of the Moscow Congress.

d) The Ninth Convention of the Communist Party in the United States in resolution 9, page 53, states that the "Communist Party in the United States commits itself to carrying on the daily practical and political tasks ... as embodied in the Sixth World Congress of the Communist International and in the resolutions of its Seventh Congress."

e) George Dimitrov at the Moscow Congress told the American delegates to organize two great fronts or false faces for Communism: one a League against War and

Fascism, the other a Farmer-Labor Party. [16] The Executive Secretary of the Communist Party of the United States on his return from the Congress obeyed the two Moscow orders and pleaded for these two very fronts. [17] The first front is now called "The American League for Peace and Democracy."

f) The American Communist Party of the United States is so much under the orders of Moscow that it is obliged under its constitution of the Communist International to "pay regularly, affiliation dues to the Executive Committee of the Communist International of Moscow." [18]

g) The Communist Party of the United States is so much under the control of Moscow that Article 34 of the Constitution states the Communist Party of the United States can convene a "Congress, ordinary and special only with the consent of the Executive Committee of the Communist International of Moscow."

h) On the occasion of the 20th anniversary of the Communist Revolution in Russia, the Communists of New York inducted 3,000 new members, who rose with clenched fists and pledged themselves to "Sovietize America." The very fact that they honor Stalin and his despotic régime is a proof of their alliance with his purges and his revolution. As Earl Browder wrote: "The defense of the Soviet Union aids the revolutionary movement throughout the world." [19]

[16] Op. cit., PP. 34. 45.
[17] Earl Browder, *What Is Communism?* pp. 112, 179.
[18] Article 33
[19] *What is Communism?* p. 173.

i) At the New York State investigation of Communist activities, June 30, 1938, Earl Browder was asked: "Is the Communist Party of the United States, a part and parcel of the Communist International in Moscow, a worldwide organization looking to the teachings of Marx, Engels, Lenin, and Stalin?"

Answer: "That is correct."

j) Next Browder was asked if he ever vetoed a single order which came from Moscow!

Answer: "Everything we ever had to pass upon we agreed with." He also admitted that the official Communist paper in the United States receives its cables free from Moscow and that in January 1938, the Communist Party of the United States paid his expenses to Moscow.

And if you doubt their revolutionary intentions in America then let me cite the Communist testimony before a special committee of the United States House of Representatives, 71st Congress, Report No. 2290. The then and present Chairman of the Communist Party of the United States, W. Z. Foster, was being questioned by the government.

Q."... the workers in this country look upon the Soviet Union as their country, is that right?"

A. "The more advanced workers do."

Q. "Look upon the Soviet Union as their country?"

A. "Yes."

Q. "They look upon the Soviet flag as their flag?"

A. "The workers of this country ... have only one flag and that is the red flag...."

Q. "... are the communists in this country opposed to our Republican form of government?"

A. "The capitalist democracy -- most assuredly...."

Q. "And they desire to overthrow it through revolutionary methods?"

A. "I would like to read from the program of the Communist International. ... The conquest of power by the proletariat does not mean peaceful capturing ... by means of a parliamentary majority ... the violence of the bourgeoisie can only be suppressed by the stern violence of the proletariat."

Q. "You take your orders from the Third International, do you?"

A. " ... The Communist International is a world party, based upon the mass parties in the respective countries. It works out its policy by the mass principles of these parties in all its deliberations ... when a decision is arrived at ... the workers, with their customary sense of proletarian discipline, accept [it] and put [it] into effect."

Q. "Do the Communists in this country advocate world revolution?"

A. "Yes...."

If it be red-baiting to bring out these facts, then where lies America's right to self-preservation? Is the doctor who takes out a ruptured appendix an appendix-baiter? Is the judge who sentences a murderer to prison a criminal-baiter? Is the father who defends his wife and children from a burglar's violence a burglar-baiter? Incidentally, why does no one ever think of calling the Communists Fascist-baiters?

If then, the Communist Party of the United States pays dues to Moscow, holds its Congresses only by its favors, and sends its head to Moscow to become a member of the Presidium of World Communism, it follows that its new tactics, dictated by the Communist International of Moscow and the Seventh Congress, will be carried out to the letter in the United States. And such is the case.

The Seventh World Congress told the Communists not to openly talk revolution but to win the masses to their side by using partial slogans, and then, by boring from within, seize leadership and start the revolution. The Communist Party of the United States is doing this very thing.

In the last Presidential election, the Communist Party of the United States published what is called "The Communist Election Platform." Its "partial slogans" were the following, none of which represent the essence of Communism any more than they represent the essence of any political party:

1. "Put Americans back to work. Provide jobs and a living wage for all." Certainly every American is in favor of this plank. In fact in 1891 Leo XIII advocated a living wage. A living wage is not the essence of Communism, for if it were, Communism would pay a living wage in Russia, which it does not do.

2. "Provide unemployment insurance, old-age pensions and social security for all." This is a plank in practically

every political platform in the world, and if Communists were interested in social security for all, it would not carry on "blood purges" in Russia.

3. "Save the young generation." To read this plank one would almost think that the other political parties were hanging the young from apple trees.

4. "Free the farmers from debts, unbearable tax burdens, and foreclosures. Guarantee the land to those who till the soil." Now the fact is that Communism in practice does not guarantee the land to those who till it. Article 6 of its Russian Constitution declares it belongs to the *State*.

5. "The rich hold the wealth of the country. Make the rich pay." Certainly the rich must pay what is just, and must realize that the use of wealth is for the common good;" but this is really absurd coming from a party where the red leaders receive 12,000 rubles a month and the average worker 225 rubles.

6. "Defend and extend democratic rights and civil liberties. Curb the Supreme Court." This plank is explained as follows: "We champion the unrestricted freedom of speech, press, and radio and assembly and the right to organize and strike." This too comes with ill grace from those who deny these very liberties in Russia. Notice it says nothing about freedom of religion. For example, Article 125 of the Russian Constitution allows freedom of speech, press, radio, and assembly on condition that they support the Communist Party. In other words, they want in America the very right they deny to others in Russia. Furthermore, they advocate the right to strike here, but

Article 131 of the Russian Constitution forbids it.

7. "Full rights for the Negro people." Certainly, everyone is in favor of this plank, but again it comes with ill grace from those who use the Negro only to further their revolutionary ends. As the Official Labor Journal of Russia puts it: "The fundamental difference between the political parties of Western Europe and us, is that we have only one possibility: one party is in power and all the others are in prison." [20]

8. "Keep America out of war by keeping war out of the world." The trick in this plank is this: Communism is opposed to all wars against Communism but is in favor of inciting civil wars among nations so as to make it easier for them to seize power. [21]

These planks are the "partial-slogans" which communism advances when there is no revolutionary upsurge." Not one of these planks is communistic. They may be planks of any political party. Why then does Communism use them? In order to create a "false front" to win over the masses, and then gradually indoctrinate them with revolutionary philosophy and action. The great pity is that so many are fooled by this "front." Too many simple-minded people think Communism is harmless because it uses harmless planks. One might just as well say a burglar is harmless because he comes in the front door. There have even been some college students who sent me this election platform saying: "This is Communism. You see it

[20] Troud, November 13, 1927.
[21] Oficial Program, 48.

Does not believe in confiscating property; it does not preach violence; it does not promote civil wars, it does not 'liquidate' or murder those who oppose it." What these students forget is that this "front" of Communism is no more Communism than a front window is a house. What then is Communism? For its real platform and its intentions, one must not go to its "front" but to its Official Program. There one reads:

"Between capitalist society and Communist society, a period of revolutionary transformation intervenes, during which the one changes into the other." The election platform says nothing about the revolution extending into the domain of property, but the Official Program makes this statement: "The proletarian revolution, however, signifies the forcible invasion of the proletariat into the domain of property." [22] Further developing its attitude towards property, the Program on page 44 goes on to state: "In carrying out all these tasks of the dictatorship of the proletariat the following postulates must be borne in mind: The complete abolition of private property in land." In the preceding pages, the Official Program goes into detail concerning the abolition of private productive capital, and on page 40, under the title of Industry, Transportation & Communication Services, uses the word "confiscation" three times, under Agriculture uses the word "confiscation" three times, under the word Housing uses the word "confiscation" once. The word "confiscation," however, is not used once in the election

[22]Pp. 34. 35.

platform. The omission is for very obvious reasons. Communism knows that it could not make any headway in the United States if it immediately began by advocating the confiscation of productive private property.

The Official Program next goes on to speak of the seizure of government power. "The conquest of power by the proletariat is the necessary condition to precede the growth of the socialist forms of economy." [23] Naturally, the friends of the government, whom the Official Program calls the bourgeoisie or Fascists, will resist any attempt on the part of the Communists to overthrow the government. The Official Program takes note of this and states on page 36: "The bourgeoisie can be suppressed only by the stern violence of the proletariat. The conquest of power by the proletariat is the violent overthrow of bourgeois power, the destruction of the capitalist state apparatus." [24]

The Communists now advance a different explanation of violence. Testifying before the New York Committee, June 30, 1938, Mr. Browder said that violence would not be practiced by the Communists but by those who resisted its progressivism. Of all the nonsense that has ever been spoken this comes first. When we put that theory of Browder's into practice, we will arrest the farmer for resisting the chicken thief; we will imprison the father for resisting the burglar. If ten thugs attack a woman, she, as the "reactionary minority," must be blamed for their

[23] P. 35
[24] P. 36, 37.

violence, but not the thugs. She brought it on herself.

Finally, although the "front" says nothing about religion, the Official Program states on page 53, "One of the most important tasks of the cultural revolution affecting the wide masses is the task of systematically and unswervingly combating religion -- the opium of the people." It furthermore states that Communism "carries on anti-religious propaganda with all the means at its command, and reconstructs the whole of its educational work on the basis of scientific materialism."

This disparity between the election platform and the Official Program is not an evidence of the change of objectives in Communism, but only a change of objectives in tactics. "Tactics change," said the Seventh Congress, "but the goal of the Communist International, namely, revolution, remains unchanged." The election platform with its harmless and vague proposals is the Trojan Horse; the Official Program is its wooden stomach filled with the revolutionists. The election platform is its smoke-screen; the Official Program is its ammunition. Modern shells, intended to penetrate armor plate, are made of the hardest steel, but they are provided with a soft metal point which, in striking the armor, composes an alloy with the substance and thus facilitates the penetration. In like manner, the Democratic Front and the election platform are the soft metal points to penetrate our national armor, and subject us, in the language of the Secretary of the Communist Party of the United States, "to Soviet Power." Even the head officials of the Communist Party in the

United States are "fronts." The real power behind the throne is not Browder, but Jack Stachel and Alex Bittelman.

Because Communism does not talk about revolution, it does not follow it disbelieves in revolution. The Moscow orders were not to talk revolution but to make it. Its front is only a lie to deceive the masses whom it hopes to lead to the "revolutionary seizure of power." It is not interested exclusively in bettering laboring conditions, in securing higher wages, or in the betterment of the poor. If all these were perfect, it would not be satisfied unless we were Bolshevized. The Communist Party promises these things to the worker in the language of one of its leaders to make revolution" in which the "Communist Party acts as the organizer and guide." [25]

The Right Hon. Winston S. Churchill, M.P., in his book, *Great Contemporaries*, has defined Communism with full knowledge of the facts:

"Communism is not only a creed. It is a plan of campaign. A communist is not only the holder of certain opinions; he is the pledged adept of a well-thought-out means of enforcing them. The anatomy of discontent and revolution has been studied in every phase and aspect, and a veritable drill book prepared in a scientific spirit for subverting all existing institutions. The method of enforcement is as much a part of the communist faith as the doctrine itself. At first, the time-honored principles of Liberalism and Democracy are invoked to shelter the

---

[25] Earl Browder, *War Is Communism?* p. 163.

infant organism. Free speech, the right of public meeting, every form of lawful political agitation, and constitutional right are paraded and asserted. Alliance is sought with every popular movement towards the left.

"The creation of a mild Liberal or Socialist regime in some period of convulsion is the first milestone. But no sooner has this been created than it is to be overthrown. Woes and scarcity resulting from confusion must be exploited. Collisions, if possible attended with bloodshed, are to be arranged between the agents of the New Government and the working people. Martyrs are to be manufactured. An apologetic attitude in the rulers should be turned to profit. Pacific propaganda may be made the mask of hatreds never before manifested among men. No faith need be, indeed may be, kept with non-communists. Every act of goodwill, of tolerance, of conciliation, of mercy, of magnanimity on the part of Government or Statesmen, is to be utilized for their ruin. Then when the time is ripe and the moment opportune, every form of lethal violence from mob revolt to private assassination must be used without stint or compunction. The citadel will be stormed under the banners of Liberty and Democracy; and once the apparatus of power is in the hands of the Brotherhood, all opposition, all contrary opinions must be extinguished by death. Democracy is but a tool to be used and afterwards broken; Liberty but a sentimental folly unworthy of the logician. The absolute rule of a self-chosen priesthood according to the dogmas it has learned by rote is to be imposed upon mankind without mitigations progressively forever. All this, set out in prosy textbooks, written also in blood in the history of several powerful nations, is the communist's faith and purpose. To be forewarned should be to be forearmed!"

Communism will not tell us that it intends a revolution; nor will it deny it. It refuses to assert its revolutionary character, for America would disown it in two minutes; it refuses to deny it, for Moscow would disown it in one minute. That is why it is the greatest deceit ever foisted on the public. Its own leader Lenin has said: "It is a matter of absolute indifference if three-quarters of the population of the world should be wiped out, so long as the other quarter is made Communist." [26]

The tactics which will endanger American democracy more than anything else in the future will be the tactics of the Popular Front, or the United Front, or what is now called the Democratic Front. The Popular Front means the union of Communism with any progressive group or party to defeat a conservative or those who oppose Communism. Thus the Popular Front in Spain, of which the Communists boasted they were the "vanguard," was composed of Left-Wing Republicans, Syndicalists, Socialists, and Anarchists. While organizing the Popular Front the Communists in the country are instructed to unite parties on the widest possible bases, namely an attack on Fascism, which to Communism means anti-Communism. The Democratic Front never means that Communism has substituted class collaboration for class conflict. It believes in the latter but

[26] *Letter of Lenin*, edited by Hill and Madie.

also believes that class collaboration is the best way to attain its revolutionary ends. The Secretary of the Communist Party says that the Popular Front "will be neither Communist nor anti-Communist." There is the reason why all Americans must oppose the Democratic Front. A political party that is neither Communist nor anti-Communist is a party that is unwilling to state its un-American movements.

When Browder was brought face to face, during the McNaboe Joint Legislative Committee, on June 30, 1938, with his revolutionary writings of a few years ago, he said that now he would not put it that way. But if he did not mean now what he wrote a few years ago, how do we know he will mean in a few years what he says now? He believed in revolution yesterday, he believes in democracy today, but tomorrow, unless he breaks with Stalin, he will believe in revolution again.

The *Brooklyn Daily Eagle* shrewdly commented on Browder's testimony as follows:

"Earl Browder's appearance on the witness stand at the hearings of the McNaboe Joint Legislative Committee on the Administration and Enforcement of the Law was highly diverting. We hope the general secretary of the Communist party in the United States did not really think he was fooling anybody.

"It should be perfectly clear that his alleged 'views as of today should be taken with a grain of salt. He and his fellow agitators, having awakened to the fact that talk of a soviet revolution here leaves the great rank and file of every-day Americans cold, have merely changed their approach. Now they purr about democracy, free speech, and the like. It is sheer hypocrisy. Soviet Russia -- and that means the Communists here, for they admittedly abide by all of Moscow's decisions -- has absolutely no use for either democracy or free speech. If communism ever got in the saddle here, it would mean dictatorship, pure and simple, with secret police, blood purges, and all the Moscow doings. Incidentally, they are the same evils which exist under fascism, too, which the Communists are constantly damning. Such is the way of totalitarianism, no matter under what label it operates.

"Browder as a democrat is just a joke. Americans, fortunately, can read and they know what is going on in Russia today. And they know that's what Browder stands for or he would not be Stalin's fair-haired boy in the United States."

The Communists appealed to the Catholics to help them further Moscowizing the United States. The answer of the Catholics is: "We appeal to you to forget Moscow and be Americans." In the language of M. Le Cour Grandmaison we say to the Communists:

"If the hand you hold out to us is that of the starving, we will give you bread both of body and soul; if that of the wounded, we will bear on our shoulders this fraternal sorrow; if that of the blind, we will guide you towards the light; if that of the despairing disinherited, we will give you peace, joy, hope and love; but if the hand that you offer is that of the traitor, of the seducer, of the enemy of souls, then in the name of Christ who saved our souls with His Blood, we will reject your gesture."

The tactics are designed solely to deceive. They will fool a few of our countrymen, but very few. No American agrees with Browder who, on June 30, 1938, testified: "We hope New York instead of Moscow will be the center of the Communist International someday." Americans love the honest man; that is why they have no fear of the sword. But they dislike the deceiver, the knave, or the one who conquers by stealth. These very tactics Communism is using now were used centuries ago, when a nervous man twitching nervously at a money bag, stole down a Jerusalem hillside. Crossing a brook, he turned to his followers and said: "He whom I shall kiss, that is He. Lay hold of Him." And Judas then threw his arms about the neck of Our Blessed Lord and blistered His lips with a kiss. Why did he use the kiss? Because he knew there was something so Divine and Sacred about Our Blessed Lord that He could be overcome only by some mark of affection.

In like manner, why do Communists use the kiss of the Democratic Front? Why do they use the kiss of the "tactics?" Because they know there is something so God-given and so sacred about national institutions that they must preface their overthrow by some sign of love. They know some things are so good that they can be betrayed only by a good sign. And so they blister our national cheek with a kiss.

It is just that kiss that made Judas the most ignominious man in human history and it is his direct descendants who turn our blood cold. Their tactics, deceits, and ruses to gain wicked ends revolt all noble hearts and honest minds. One can know the tactics of Communism, and its promises, peruse its propaganda, attend its inflammatory sessions, glance into its anti-religious museums, scan its atheistic literature, read its hymns of hate against God and fellowman, and yet one will never be convinced that there is no God. But because one knows its tactics, one is convinced of one thing, and that is, that there is a Devil!

Chapter VII

Patriotism

The treatise on Patriotism in the writings of the greatest philosopher of all times, St. Thomas Aquinas, is to be found under the subject of "Piety." This at first may seem strange to those who think of piety as pertaining only to love of God. But once it is remembered that love of neighbor is inseparable from love of God, then love of our fellow citizens is a form of piety. In these days when so many subversive activities are at work, a reminder of the necessity of loving our country is very much to the point. The subject is here considered in the light of three movements alien to the spirit of Americanism, namely Fascism, Nazism, and Communism.

Fascism, Nazism, and Communism have some characteristics in common: all subject the masses to a dictator; all assert that personal rights can be modified or destroyed by the State; all permit only one party which is identical with the State; and all suppress liberty of speech, press, and assembly, except when used to support the unique party. It is very important to keep these similarities in mind, particularly the fact that all have dictators.

But there are some differences between Fascism and Communism. Neither Fascism nor Nazism put all productive property in the hands of the State; Communism does.

Secondly, Fascism and Nazism do not scruple to resort to violence to maintain their dictatorship; Communism makes violence and class struggle the very soul of its dictatorship. Thirdly, Fascism tolerates religion, Nazism persecutes it, but Communism is essentially atheistic and its Program states that one of the principal tasks of the revolution is that of "systematically and unswervingly combating religion, the 'opium of the people." Finally, Fascism and Nazism defend tradition; Communism uproots it. It is immediately evident that neither Fascism nor Communism has any place in American life, for both dictatorships, violence and the suppression of political liberties, run counter to our traditions and our history.

The term "Fascist" is never used politically by Communism, but to signify what is anti-Communist. The best description of the way the Communist uses it was given by *America*.

"As a term of opprobrium, the latest American lingo has no word to equal *Fascist*. Since the term is used in so many senses, we are in deep doubt as to what usage is making it mean. We can, however, glean some of its meanings from those who hurl it. We should judge that a Fascist is an ogre, a monster, so horrible that to name it means to shiver at it. To the little Red schoolboy, the exacting public school teacher, and likewise the policeman, are Fascists. To his elders, the owner, whoever he be, of a factory is a Fascist. Most probably, the superintendent, if hired by the owner is one also. Every capitalist cannot but be a Fascist; and if he be one, his secretary and his contented clerks are likewise Fascist. To the pink Catholic, the priest is, at least, a suspected Fascist, as is the Bishop and the Pope. And sometimes, strangely, the editors of this Review are condemned as Fascists.

"As far as we can discover, anyone may be called a Fascist who: is a ruthless dictator in Germany, Italy, and Nationalist Spain; exercises any authority that irks you, no matter over what he exercises authority; enjoys wealth, even a competence that gives him little luxuries; says that there should be law and order in the United States, enforced by the constituted guardians; intimates that violence and obstruction are not fit tactics for labor unions to use; advocates the slightest reduction in Government doles; in brief, anyone who does not accept the Marxist concept of government and society.

"So comprehensive is the term Fascist in the current American language that it may be applied to all except those who openly or covertly profess Communism. That is, it is synonymous with anti-Communist. So disgraceful is it, that public officials shrink from being accused of it. But to be absolved from being considered a Fascist, a denial is not sufficient. It is required that one profess an undiluted, or at least a diluted, Communism.

"It would seem almost too late to attempt to rescue the true and original meaning of Fascist and Fascism. No American, loyal to the American system of democracy, can be really a Fascist, for Fascism in its technical and restricted meaning is a negation of American democracy. Nor can a Catholic accept the essential theory of

Government Fascism, that is, a totalitarianism which does not recognize human and spiritual values outside the state, and except as conferred or allowed by the State. Likewise, the American and the Catholic could not adopt the theory of Social Fascism, defined by Father LaFarge in his pamphlet *Fascism* to be 'the attempt to fix the relations of social or economic groups by the use of force, particularly governmental force, in the interests of economic dictatorship.

"Taking these definitions as accurate, one concludes that there are few Fascists in the United States. And yet, the Communist propagandists have been so successful that they have tagged the name Fascist on all with whom they disagree, that means, on all authentic Americans."

It now remains to dissipate two clever tricks of Communist propaganda: the first is the implication that if you are not a Communist, you are a Fascist; and secondly, that Communism is democracy.

I. Communism has been attempting lately and with great success to obscure the similarities between itself and Fascism. It does this by giving words a meaning which is not found in our dictionaries. It never speaks of Fascism as being similar to Communism in its most un-American and un-democratic aspects, namely dictatorship and suppression of liberties. Rather it defines Fascism as "war" or as "exploiting blood-sucking capitalism." By thus obscuring the essential resemblances between Fascism and Communism it succeeds in getting childish minds to believe that Fascism is wicked and Communism is good, and that only Fascists are in favor of war and the suppression of the worker.

Now, as a matter of fact, the spirit of war is just as common to Communism as it is to Fascism, otherwise, Communists would not maintain the largest army in the world. Furthermore, the crushing of the workers is even less the spirit of capitalism than it is the spirit of Communism, as the lumber camps and blood purges of Russia so well prove. Changing of definitions must not obscure the reality. Because I am not a Communist, it does not follow that I am a Fascist or for war or the "slaughtering of the workers," any more than because I do not like caviar does it follow that I must necessarily be mad about spaghetti. The two are not mutually exclusive, hence I can be a dozen different things without being a Communist; for example, I can be an American. Be not therefore deluded by slogans or maneuvered into believing that if you do not accept Communism, you must accept Fascism.

Here is the infallible way to discover a Communist inspired lecture, newspaper, periodical, society organization, broadcast, or league: if it condemns only Fascism but never Communism, you can be sure it is Russian, not American, for America has no use for either. Thousands of college students every year are duped into a demonstration by Democratic fronts of Communism, never seeming to realize that America is just as much opposed to a Communist dictator as to a Fascist dictator. This ruse of making it appear as if there were only one enemy is the clever way the other enemy uses to put us to sleep. The tactics of Communism in relation to Fascism are very much like those of the prizefighter who whispered to his opponent in a clinch that his shoestring was untied, and then as he let down his guard, cracked him into oblivion. So too Communism says: "Look out, you are about to trip yourself on Fascism," and then as we prepare to battle it, Communism worms its way in for the kill. It is all well and good to keep Fascism out of American life, but it ill becomes the pot to call the kettle black. Undoubtedly the proper thing to do is keep both out.

This brings us to the problem of the best way to keep Fascism out of American life. The answer is: "Keep out Communism." The reason is simple. Fascism arises always as a reaction against Communism. Historically, Fascism did not arise as a separate and independent movement; it rose as a reaction to Communism and its threats of revolution. The only way a government can put down a revolution is by centralizing authority, as it does in case of war; this produces a dictatorship. That is how Fascism arose in Hungary after Bela Kun took his orders from Moscow and started a revolution; that is how it brought Mussolini's black shirts to Italy and how it brought Hitler to Germany, and how it started Mosley in England and La Rocque in France. In the nature of things, nothing else but Fascism can result when Communism begins its threats of violence and revolution. The natural, healthy, instinctive reaction of Western man is against a mode of life which believes revolution is the only path to order.

The world takes one look at Russia with the millions of lives it took to establish Communism and then asks if it is worth the cost. Its desolation and its horror frighten the world, and Fascism becomes the product of that fear. A strong central government with autocratic powers necessarily arose to protect itself against the Russian way of life. Fascism then is not first, but Communism. Fascism is its reaction. If then the Communists want us to keep out Fascism, the best way to do it is to keep out Communism. If we do not want to use rat poison, we must keep out the rats; if we do not want an anti-Communistic dictator, then we must not want a Communistic dictator; if we do not want to throw away our food, then we must not sprinkle it with either the Paris green of the Communistic Popular Front or the Moscow red of the dictatorship over the proletariat. If we do not allow Communism to upset our national life, then we will not have to worry about Fascism which will arise to put it down. The Communists are beginning to realize this after their failure in Spain. They had planned the revolution in France at exactly the same time as in Spain, according to their "Confidential Report No. 3 of Madrid." Why did they not start the revolution in France? Probably because they feared a popular reaction. It will be this fear of a national protest against its revolution which will make Communism, by slow evolution become Fascism, and attempt to establish a dictatorship without a bloody revolution. In any case, if we think of Communism as Soviet Fascism we will not be fooled by propaganda.

More concretely, two safe guides for Americans are these:

a) Do not join *any organization which condemns Fascism but is silent about Communism*, true Americanism is opposed to both. This rule will keep us out of the "American League for Peace and Democracy" and the "American Youth Congress," and the "League for Spanish Democracy."

b) Use the term "Soviet Fascism" to describe Communism and you nullify its tactics.

II. A second trick against which America must be on guard is the Communist one of identifying Communism with democracy. This may be done either directly by saying that Communism is democracy or indirectly by saying that the world must choose between Fascism and Communism. The truth is that the interests of democracy lie neither in an alliance with Fascism or Communism.

But why does Communism talk of itself in terms of democracy? Certainly, a regime such as exists in Russia is not a democracy, for only $1 \frac{1}{2}$ percent of the population belong to the Communist Party, and this $1 \frac{1}{2}$ percent control the other $98 \frac{1}{2}$ percent. Furthermore, no rival parties are tolerated; the citizens enjoy the secret ballot, but they may vote only for the nominees of the Communist Party and for no other; they may never dissent with its decisions for dissent is defined as "counter-revolution." But the dissent of a minority is the essence of democracy. All the Communist's talk about Communism being on the side of democracy is a little unconvincing when one recalls that the Russian Communists gained power by stabbing a provisional government in the back after an election in which the Communist candidates were defeated six to one. Stranger still is that after twenty years of so called democracy, Russia is still supporting a dictator who has "liquidated" everyone who opposed his will. Why then, do they use the term "democracy" to define their dictatorship over the proletariat? They use it, first of all, because they want to court the approval of the democratic nations, such as France, England, and America, and of course, the best way to do this is to say that Communism is democracy. This meant Communism had to swallow all the wicked things it said about democracy, but it was willing to do this to win allies against Italy, Germany, and Japan. Another reason for the Communist's use of the term "democracy," is that Communism is possessed of an envious hatred of liberty and wellbeing which their rationalized lunacy has failed to achieve, and they have left only a depraved desire to drag us down into the same pit into which they themselves have fallen.

More important is the meaning which the Communists attach to the term "democracy." When they say "democracy" they cannot possibly mean American democracy, otherwise, they would not abuse the privileges which democracy gives them in order to destroy it. There is more in common between Fascism and Communism than between Communism and a democracy, and no one knows it better than Communism.

It is not difficult to discover what Communism means by democracy if we understand the tactics ordered by the Seventh Congress, namely, worm your way into democratic institutions by using their slogans.

The first point to be kept clearly in mind is that when Communism uses the term "democracy" it does not mean a system of government such as we have in America, but a dictatorship such as exists in Russia; "We Communists are unswerving upholders of *Soviet Democracy*, the great prototype of which is the proletarian dictatorship in the Soviet Union."[1] Communism here deliberately uses a word but gives it an entirely different meaning. When it says democracy it means dictatorship and in particular, that kind that presently enslaves Russia.

The documents now go on to tell us that Soviet democracy is inseparable from revolution, the overthrow of our present government by violence,[2] the substitution of a dictator, the confiscation of property, and Socialism. "This Soviet Democracy presupposes the victory of the proletarian revolution, the conversion of private property as the means of production into public property, the embarking of the overwhelming majority of people on the road to Socialism."[3] But this is not democracy as understood by America, for democracy does not mean revolution, it does not mean confiscation of private property and it does not mean Socialism; but that is

[1]Dimitrov, *The Working Class Against Fascism*, p. 126.
[2]Program, p. 36.
[3] Dimitrov, p. 126.

precisely what democracy means to a Communist.

Now that Communism has given a new meaning to democracy, and identified it with Soviet Socialism, it, of course, had to find an epithet for those who believe in American democracy. The epithet was easy to find; namely, "Fascist." Americans who understand by democracy, not dictatorship after revolution, but the enjoyment of liberties guaranteed by our constitution, are called "Fascists."[4] It now becomes clear that Communism smiles on democracy only as part of a revolutionary technique dictated by Marx and Lenin. America, of course, is willing to admit that Communism, after destroying Russia in the revolution, has done much to put Russia on its feet again, but we Americans have no desire to be reduced to the sad condition of Russia in 1917 in order to receive the blessings of Stalin.

When Moscow ordered its agents in America to talk about democracy, it was only natural for the old-guard Communists to feel that Communism had become soft. "After all, why talk about democracy, when we mean Communism?" they were asking. Moscow answered this objection about fear of launching democratic slogans: "And the circumstance that even today we must still make reference to fear in our ranks, of launching positive democratic slogans indicates how little our comrades have mastered the Marxist-Leninist method of approaching such an important problem of tactics. Some say that the struggle for democratic rights may divert the workers from

[4]Dimitrov, p. 44

the struggle for proletarian dictatorship. It may not be amiss to recall what Lenin said on this question: 'It would be a fundamental mistake to suppose that the struggle for democracy can divert the proletariat from the Socialist revolution or obscure, or overshadow it. [5]

The meaning is clear: When Communism talks democracy it means revolution. Or more concretely, the Communist's interest in American liberty is the liberty to end our liberty by revolution, violence, and dictatorship over the proletariat. The use of the term "democracy" is therefore only a ruse. They use the term "democracy" as a "front" and a "front," as the name implies, is only a façade.[6] Certainly if Communism and democracy were identical, why were the Communists warned during their Seventh Congress not to forget the "fundamental differences between Communism and democracy, namely "the revolution, the dictatorship of the proletariat in the form of the Soviet power, and the defense of the bourgeois fatherland, Russia?" The Communist leaders had to do that, lest some stupid idiot think that Communism was really democratic. The same Congress went on to say that those who think that when Communism is talking democracy it has forgotten the revolutionary character of Communism are "downright scoundrels." A few lines later, it tells the Communists that if they think that by this "new united front tactics," "Communism is capitulating to Social-Democracy," they

[5]Dimitrov, p. 129.
[6]Manuilsky, *The Word of the Seventh Congress*, p. 65.

are "hopeless idiots."[7]

In this same connection let those parties, born of American liberty, be careful about the support given to them by the Communists. They seek to form a "Democratic Front" with other parties, but this is only a temporary alliance which in the end will serve purposes of revolution. The Resolution of August 20, 1935, gave the following order for Communist Parties in the United States and throughout the world: "The unification of social-democratic parties or any particular organization with the Communist Party should be subject to the recognition of the *necessity of the revolutionary overthrow of the existing order* and the *installation of the* Dictatorship of the proletariat under the form of the Soviet." [8] The orders from Moscow in the Seventh Congress were to pass "from the position of class collaboration so *with* the bourgeoisie to the position of class struggle *against* the bourgeoisie." [9]

Certainly, it has never been in the atmosphere of democracy to form a party which will first unite with a class and then struggle against it, for nothing would be greater proof of the baseness and insincerity of its motives. Communism did not begin as a democracy, nor can it end as one. It was not established in Russia by a spontaneous uprising of workers, but by a conspiracy in which revolutionists manipulated the masses of deserting soldiers and hungry peasants through promises which

[7]Manuky. -59
[8]*Pravda,* August 6, 1935
[9]Dimitrov, p. 122

they never kept and never could keep. Such a dictatorship cannot be put over on the American people even though Communism does wear the mask and babble the language of democracy. Dictatorship to America is despotism, whether it be the dictatorship of German Fascism or Soviet Fascism. We have a Bill of Rights in this country, and if the Communists think Americans do not prize those rights, then let them try to take it away. It is a very curious thing indeed that just as soon as anyone opposes the Communist's propaganda, the Communists are the very first to appeal to our democracy and our Bill of Rights. In other words, they invoke the blessings of democracy in order to give us the curse of a Soviet dictatorship. They appeal to "Freedom of speech" to attack our government and its courts, and yet will not allow a similar right in the land of Soviet Fascism. They demand the very rights here which they are refused there. This creates the problem of the right of free speech. How far may it be employed? To what extent may it be used? Does it apply to anyone who wishes to dissent with any person or policy in politics? Most certainly. Does it mean that we must allow the Communists and Fascists and all who believe in dictators to state their arguments? Most certainly. But does this mean that there is to be no limit whatever to their invoking freedom of speech and freedom of assembly? It certainly does not. Freedom of speech does not mean freedom to advocate abolition of freedom of speech. Hence democratic governments can tolerate Communists and Fascists so long as they are weak enough to be negligible and as long as they have no hope of success. But if they become strong enough to use their constitutional liberty to destroy liberty: to use force to destroy government; to use democracy to destroy democracy as the Nazis did in Germany, then they present a challenge which no government can ignore.

The rights of freedom of speech are not unlimited as the radicals imagine. There is a limit to its exercise and it is this: One may never invoke a right to destroy it. I have the right to property, but I may not invoke that right to steal your property. In like manner, Communists may enjoy freedom of speech, but only on condition that they do not invoke it in order to destroy it, i.e., establish a régime such as there is in Russia and Germany, where one may use it only to praise a dictator. Let the Communists assure us that they will not bludgeon us into lip service of Stalin, and will not take away our democratic right to disagree with their confiscation and violence; let them assure us that they will break off relations with Communist Moscow and live as Americans for America, and we will allow them the freedom of speech. Then they will invoke the right to preserve it and glorify it, but that is not Communism, it is democracy!

What is Americanism? This question was not asked some years ago, partly because the rest of the world believed, at least in principle, in democracy; partly because we were spared from the missionary activities of foreign governments which would impose their governmental systems upon us; and partly because dictatorships had not arisen to challenge our basic political philosophy. But now that democracy is challenged, Americans are forced to inquire into their national past, to seek out an answer to that question.

Consciously or unconsciously our citizens are grouping themselves around the only two possible answers. The first answer is that the essence of Americanism is revolution; the second answer is that the essence of Americanism consists in the recognition of the sacredness of human personality.

The revolutionary theory:

The Communists in their attempt to justify another revolution are rewriting American history to suit the dialectics of Marx and Lenin. Their argument is this: America began with a revolution, the real descendants, then, of our national forefathers are those who believe in revolution. But the Communists believe in revolutionary theory and practice; therefore they are the true Americans.

In support of this thesis, the Secretary of the Communist Party in the United States writes in his work, *What is Communism?* "The revolutionary tradition is the heart of Americanism... We, Communists, claim the revolutionary traditions of Americanism. We are the only ones who consciously continue these traditions and apply them to the problems of the day. *We are the Americans and Communism is the Americanism of the 20th Century.* ... Our American giants were the international incendiaries of their day. They inspired revolutions throughout the world." [10] "The reactionaries will rise up against us; they will denounce us as Reds, and revolutionists. Of this, we need not be afraid. Revolution is the essence of the American tradition." [11]

Before passing on to the other theory concerning the essence of Americanism it might be well to investigate the value of the Communist theory. Is it logical? There probably is no one, who uses even one of his intellectual lobes, who cannot see the fallacy of the argument. First of all, to argue that because the Communists believe in revolution, therefore they are the heirs of the Revolutionary War, is just as stupid as to say that every American who wears a red coat is a descendant of an English soldier. Furthermore, since when does the Revolutionary War give a man a right to be revolutionary? Does it give you and me the right to drive through red traffic lights, even though they are of the Communist color? And why should revolution be the unique right of the Communist? Why should it not be the right of everyone, for that is the meaning of revolution? Then every fool is entitled to be revolutionary who would turn our country into a great free-for-all.

The plain fact is that Communists in America are presently attempting to rewrite American history, as they are rewriting English and French history to prove that it fits into the dialectics evolved by Marx in the middle of the last century. Instead of reading history from sources, they

[10] Pp. 16 and 19.
[11] Browder, *Lincoln and the Communists*, F. 13.

start with Marx's materialist conception of history and make the facts fit the theory. As Browder puts it: "We have something that others lack, the key to unlock the great treasures (of history) in the scientific study of history, historical materialism, founded by Marx and Engels and developed by Lenin and Stalin." [12]

But if we are going to impose these theories upon facts, how can we be certain that the Marxist interpretation is right? Why not Spengler's interpretation? Why not Croce's? Why not Schlegel's? Why not Wells's interpretation?

If the Communist chooses to wear red glasses to look at historical facts, why is it not the privilege of others to wear pink glasses and the privilege of the pessimists to wear black glasses, and the privilege of the Nazis to wear brown glasses? The proper way to read American history is to take off all the colored glasses, and then Jefferson will not be the great "enemy of the vested interests and Hamilton the "Wall Street broker." Rather, despite their differences, both were dedicated to principles of human relationship which history has proven to be the only alternative to tyranny and terror.

The facts of history clearly prove that the Constitution of the United States was not the product of a revolution, but of basic fundamental principles of human nature common to all men, and that is why practically every provision in the Constitution is to be found in the Constitution of the

[12] *The Communist*, September, 1937

several states, many of which were written before the revolution.

It is therefore no more true to say that "Communism is twentieth-century Americanism" than it is true to say that "Fascism is twentieth-century Americanism," for America never contemplated in its Constitution a dictator, whether he be Bolshevik or Fascist. If "Communism is twentieth-century Americanism" why does the Communist Party of the United States remain affiliated to the Communist International of Moscow? Why does it pay dues to Moscow, according to Article 33 of its constitution with Moscow? Why does it agree not to hold a Congress in the United States without the permission of the executive committee of Moscow, according to Article 34 of its constitution with Moscow? Why does it allow its candidate for President in the United States to become a member of the Moscow Presidium? How they would howl if any other candidate for President of the United States were even just an honorary member of the Nazis. Why did the Communist Party of the United States send delegates to the last Moscow Congress? Why did the official organ of the Communist International of Moscow say the book of the Secretary of the Communist Party in the United States was in complete accord with the new tactics by the Communist International of Moscow? Why did the leaders of the Communist Party in the United States, on July 27 and 28, 1935, stand on their feet in Moscow and cheer "Stalin the leader of world revolution" as reported?

If an alliance with Moscow is twentieth-century Americanism; if revolution, violence, "ruthless suppression of minorities," "confiscation," "purging of the old dross of society" is twentieth-century Americanism, then how does America differ from Moscow? If America believed that Communism were twentieth-century Americanism our government would never have signed an agreement with Russia as it did in 1931, specifying that a commercial treaty did not give them a right to carry on the propaganda of the Revolutionary Third International. Russia has broken this agreement a thousand times over. It breaks it at every national convention when a representative of the Third International of Moscow attends. The reason we have done nothing about it is because the American good sense has refused and will refuse to follow any system which in one day executes seven generals of the army, three newspaper editors, two members of a cabinet. If they insist on appealing to the American Revolution we would remind them it was a political revolution against a government across a sea, and not a civil war and class struggle against one another. In any case, what was the end and purpose of the Revolutionary War? It was to keep a foreign power out of America. The real heirs of the American Revolution are therefore not the Communists, but those who in this year attempt to keep other foreign powers out of America, whether they be Fascists or Communists.

The essence of Americanism is not revolution, but the recognition of the sacredness of human personality, and the inherent inalienable rights which every man possesses independent of the State. That is why when our country began, our Founding Fathers were most anxious to find some basis for human rights, some foundation for human liberties, some guarantee of human personality which would be above encroachments of tyranny and abuse. But where find the basis for the right of a man to be his own master, captain of his own soul, free in his right to pursue his ultimate end with a free conscience? Where root and ground the right to own property as the extension of personality? Where find the rock of all liberties which would be strong enough to withstand governments and powers and States which would absorb them as the monarchies did then, and as certain dictatorships do now?

For such a foundation the Fathers looked first to England. There the theory was advanced that our liberties and rights are rooted in Parliament. This theory they rejected on the ground that if Parliament gives rights and liberties, then the Parliament can take them away.

Next they looked to France, where it was held that the liberties and rights of man are rooted in the will of the majority. The Fathers equally rejected this on the ground that if the rights of man are the gift of the majority, then the majority can take away the rights of the minority. Where find the source of the liberties and the rights of man? On what stable foundation are they to be reared? What is their source! The answer they gave was the right one. They sought the foundations of man's rights and liberties in something so sacred and so inalienable that no State, no Parliament, no dictator, no human power could ever take them away and so they rooted them in God. As the Declaration of Independence reads: "All men are endowed by the Creator with certain inalienable rights," and among these are "life, liberty and the pursuit of happiness." Note that the word used is "inalienable"; that means that rights belong to the sacredness of human personality and are not the gift of the State, or a dictator, either Fascist, Nazi, or Communist.

There was no question of ceding rights as the new constitutions of Russia and Mexico do. The only rights the citizens of those countries enjoy are those granted by the constitution. With us, it is different. Man has rights and liberties previous to any constitution, and because they are God-derived, and not man-derived, it follows that no State can ever take them away. That is why our government recognizes that the rights of man are broader than the Constitution as is stated in Amendment 9 of the Constitution, "The enumeration in the Constitution of certain rights, shall not be construed to deny or disparage others retained by the people."

In other words, man's right to own private property, man's right to educate his own family, man's right to adore God according to the dictates of his conscience, come not from the Constitution, the government, parliament, nor the will of the majority, but from God. Therefore no power on earth can take them away. This is the essence of Americanism. Now, if the essence of Americanism is the sacredness of human personality as a creature of God, who is doing most to preserve that Americanism? The schools that never mention His name?   The universities and colleges that dissolve the Deity into the latest ultimate of physics or biology? The professors who adjust their ethics to suit unethical lives?

The answer obviously is, that the forces that are building constructive Americanism are those that take a practical cognisance of the existence of God. It is the non-religious schools which are out of the tradition of Americanism; they are on the defensive. In the beginning of our national life, practically all of our schools and colleges were religious schools. It was assumed by our Constitution and by its spirit that they would be religious. The reason was obvious. If human dignity and liberty come from God, then it follows that loss of faith in Him means loss of faith in those liberties which derive from Him. If we wish to have the light we must keep the sun, if we wish to keep our forests, we must keep our trees; if we wish to keep our perfumes we must keep our flowers, and if we wish to keep our rights, then we must keep our God. It is just as vain to try to keep triangles without keeping three-sided figures, as to try to keep liberty without the spirit which makes man independent of matter and therefore free.

Catholics are taking religion so seriously in reference to our country that, rather than see God perish out of our national life, we conduct 7,950 elementary schools and

2,175 public schools, employing 58,000 and 15,000 teachers respectively. These two schools represent an investment of $750,000,000 for elementary schools, and $575,000,000 for high schools. To keep the system going we spend $58,000,000 a year on elementary schools and $10,000,000 a year on high schools and, figuring on the basis of public school costs, we save the taxpayers of the country $139,600,000 a year. Every cent of this money comes out of the pockets of Catholics, and why? Because we believe that the 2,177,000 children in elementary schools and 285,000 in high schools have a right to know the truth which makes them free. In other words, we take very seriously the Declaration of Independence which derives the rights of man from God.

In conclusion, true Americanism is the freedom of man as a divine derivative. For that reason, if we wish to keep pure Americanism, we must keep our religion. To this is to be added the important fact, that dictatorship can exist without religion, but democracy cannot The reason is that dictatorships, such as the Communistic, regard man only as a stomach to be fed by the State, or as a tool to amass wealth for the State. Put men on that level and they need religion no more than animals need religion, or a monkey-wrench needs liturgy. But to put them on that level is to de-personalize and mechanize them down to the very core of their being. A democracy needs religion, for it assumes that man has not only a stomach but also a soul which is the seat of his rights, and since that soul must be fed as well as his body, he must have religion.

Furthermore, a dictatorship can exist without religion because the unity it achieves is from the outside and not from the inside. The unity of the citizens in a Nazi or Communist régime is a forced unity. The party acts as the shepherd dogs which herd the citizens into the unity of the sheepfold by barking at their heels. It produces a unity, but it is a forced unity in which man is nothing more than an automaton or social atom.

Democracy relies not on force, but on freedom and liberty. But freedom and liberty are inseparable from responsibility, and responsibility is inseparable from conscience, and conscience is inseparable from religion.

It is our solemn duty as Catholics to be conscious of our duty to America, and to preserve its freedom by preserving its faith in God against that group that would identify revolution with America; we must protest that there are stars in our flag and not a hammer and a sickle, to remind us that the destiny of human life is beyond the implements of daily toil -- beyond the stars and the "hid battlements of eternity" with God. The Communists want the flag all red. We are willing to have a little red in it, but we want some white and blue in it too. Then the red will not stand for revolution, but for sacrifice and above all else a sacrifice inspired by the death of Him on Calvary who proved the greatest love of all. Then the blue in it will remind us that we must be loyal to America, never daring to subvert it even under the gentler name of "front."

Then the white in it will remind us that we must keep it pure and un-Moscowized. But as we talk about patriotism, it might be well to remind ourselves that in a crisis like this, perhaps even devotion to the stars and stripes is not enough to save us. We must look beyond them to other stars and stripes, namely, the stars and stripes of Christ, by Whose stars we are illumined and by Whose stripes we are healed!

Chapter VIII

Charity

The Holy Father offers something still more important as a remedy for Communism, or certainly more directly calculated to cure it," namely, the practice of charity. "We have in mind," he writes, that Christian charity, "patient and kind' which avoids all semblance of demeaning paternalism, and all ostentation: that charity which from the beginning of Christianity won to Christ the poorest of the poor, the slaves. ... And we are grateful to all those members of charitable associations, from the conferences of St. Vincent de Paul to the recent great relief organizations, which are perseveringly practicing the spiritual and corporal works of mercy. The more the workingman and the poor realize what the spirit of love animated by the virtue of Christ is doing for them, the more readily they will abandon the false persuasion that Christianity has lost its efficacy and that the Church stands on the side of the exploiters of their labor."

The Church is addressing her own children, and not alone those who have, but those who have not, for the precept of charity applies to both the rich and the poor. She is also clearly stating that the advance of Communism is in part a result of our own unfulfilled duty. If the rich hate the poor and the poor hate the rich it is because both have offended against charity: the rich by being too selfish and the poor by being too envious. The rich who exploit the poor and the poor who would violently dispossess the rich, are extremes equally wrong and therefore equally to be condemned. To both, the precept of charity must be preached.

To the Rich:

The precept of charity teaches the rich two truths: (a) that they are but stewards of wealth, (b) the necessity of being detached from their wealth out of love for the poor.

As regards the stewardship of wealth the Church says: "The rich should consider themselves only as stewards of their earthly goods, and be mindful of the account they must render of them to their Lord and Master, and value them as precious means that God has put into their hands for doing good; and let them not fail, besides, to distribute of their abundance to the poor, according to the evangelical precept. Otherwise, there shall be verified of them and their riches the harsh condemnation of St. James the Apostle: "Go to now, ye rich men; weep and howl in your miseries which shall come upon you. Your riches are corrupted and your garments are moth-eaten: your gold and silver is cankered; and the rust of them shall be for a testimony against you and shall eat your flesh like fire. You have stored up to yourselves wrath against the last day." [1]

The stewardship of wealth means that wealth is not a

[1]*Divini Redemptoris.*

possession, but a trust. Wealth is something we hold from God, and for which we must render an account; it is nothing wholly personal like an heirloom, but something functional like a university endowment: it must be used for good purposes. Wealth requires justification, and it may be justified on benevolent grounds or on aesthetic grounds. Of its benevolent use, our Lord spoke when He said to the rich young man: "Yet one thing is wanting to thee. Go sell all thou hast and give to the poor, and thou shalt have treasure in heaven. And come, follow Me." [2] Of the aesthetic use of wealth, our Lord spoke the day He praised a converted sinner for anointing His feet. She used her wealth to adorn the Temple of God which He is, for which she received the promise that her good deed would be recorded to the end of time. In this day, there are those who seeing wealth given to the adornment of God's altar condemn the Church for accepting it, as Judas on that day seeing ointment poured on the feet of the Saviour asked, "Why all this waste?"

The rich may not assume that the first claim on their money is their own comfort, or that they need give no alms until all their imaginable comforts are satisfied, or that their possessions must determine their station in life. Rather they must justify the right to be rich by being generous, by serving the poor, and adoring God. Then the poor will not hate them. It is the rich who refuse to consider themselves as stewards of their wealth who come under the warning of Our Lord: "How hardly shall

[2] Luke 18:20

they that have riches enter into the Kingdom of God;" [3] "It is easier for a camel to pass through the eye of a needle than for a rich man to enter into the kingdom of heaven. [4] The Divine Master said these things because most rich men do not possess wealth; wealth possesses them. They, therefore, do not belong to themselves; they are the prisoners of things. They have no time to think of their souls, because they are under the fear of losing their wealth, and because their power of love is completely absorbed by money. This does not mean the rich man will lose his soul because of his wealth, but he is in danger of losing it because he is selfish with it. Riches in themselves are no more of a barrier to salvation than cancer; but riches kept for personal comfort and to the utter forgetfulness of others, are among the greatest barriers to everlasting peace. The more men retain their wealth and the less conscious they are of being its administrators, the poorer they really are and the more they stand in need of God. It was the rich young man and not Jesus who went away sorrowful.

The stewardship of wealth is quite a different thing from giving to philanthropies to escape income taxes or for purposes of propaganda. It must mean for every rich Catholic a recognition of the fact that he can belong to the Church only on condition that he serve the poor. Just as a bank clerk can hold his position only on condition that he recognize his stewardship to the bank, so a wealthy man

[3]Mark 10:23
[4]Matthew 19:24

can belong to the Church only on condition that he recognize his stewardship to God. Being a steward of God does not mean relieving the poor out of esteem or pity; it does not mean aiding them as unfortunates on a lower level; it means paying court to the poor as the eminent and honorable members of the Mystical Body of Christ. The poor in the Church are the persons of distinction, and the rich *as rich* enter the Church for only one purpose, viz., to serve the poor. Our Lord came into this world not as a master, but as a servant, and with that same spirit, each one must act toward his fellowship. "By calling in the poor, the weak, the blind and the lame,"[5] the Lord filled His house, and for no other reason did He call them in but that others might be their stewards. There is no escaping the Beatitude: "Blessed are the poor in spirit, for theirs is the Kingdom of Heaven."

His Heavenly Father, He said, sent Him "to preach the Gospel *to the poor*."[6] If God sent His Son to serve the poor, then the rich can do no less. Their salvation, it may be said, is In the hands of the poor. If they keep what they have and refuse to be God's stewards, then on the last day the Judge will say to them the harshest words ever pronounced: "You have already had your reward," and what a poor reward the glory of the earth is when we must leave it in a shroud without pockets. But if the rich have borne the burdens of the poor, then their wealth is never lost; it was merely exchanged, for the Kingdom of Heaven

[5] Luke 14:21.
[6] Luke 4:18.

is for the rich who become poor, i.e., the rich who freely give to creatures that which the Creator gave to them. The privilege of the rich man is exchange. God has put into his hands goods of one kind which he may exchange for another, namely, the material for the spiritual. The sharing of wealth then is not a loss, nor a surrender, nor even a sacrifice, but a profitable transaction, for what exchange shall a man give for his soul"? Herein lies the answer to the rich who ask: "Well, why did God give me wealth if He did not intend that I should keep it and enjoy it?" He gave it in order that you might exchange it for something else.

In a certain sense, the rich have a great advantage inasmuch as God has given to them wealth of which they may charitably dispose in order to save their souls. It was precisely this idea of exchange Our Lord had in mind when He said: "Sell what you have and give alms. Make yourselves bags which grow not old, a treasure in heaven which faileth not, where no thief approacheth, nor moth corrupteth ... when thou makest a dinner or a supper, call not thy friends, nor thy brethren, nor thy kinsmen nor thy neighbors who are rich; lest perhaps they also invite thee again and a recompense be made to thee. But when thou makest a feast, call the poor, the maimed, the lame, and the blind; and thou shalt be blessed, because they have not wherewith to make recompense; for recompense shall be made at the resurrection of the just."

Until that time the Divine Master bids the rich be kind

to the poor, so that when their wealth fails them at death, the poor whom they aided, may plead for the salvation of their souls. There is exchange at its peak, and with it, the astounding revelation that in the Church, the poor can do more for the rich than the rich can do for the poor. Stewardship then means more than helping the "deserving poor," for helping the deserving poor is not charity but justice. Stewardship means helping even the undeserving poor, and that is charity!

Detachment:

The precept of charity implies not only stewardship but also the spirit of detachment. In this connection, the Holy Father bemoans the selfishness with which wealth is used to the utter forgetfulness of the poor. "When on the one hand we see thousands of the needy, victims of real misery for various reasons beyond their control, and on the other, so many around them who spend huge sums of money on useless and frivolous amusement, we cannot fail to remark with sorrow not only that justice is poorly observed, but that the precept of charity also is not sufficiently appreciated and is not a vital thing in our daily life. We desire therefore that this divine precept, this precious mark of identification left by Christ to His true disciples, be ever more fully explained by pen and mouth; this precept which teaches us to see in those who suffer Christ Himself, and would have us love our brothers as Our Divine Saviour has loved us, that is, even at the sacrifice of ourselves, and if need be, of our very life. ... To be sure of eternal life, therefore, to be able to help the poor effectively it is imperative to return to a more moderate way of life, to renounce the joys, often sinful, which the world today holds out in such abundance; to forget self for the love of neighbor." [7]

Detachment goes deeper than stewardship for it implies the renouncement of abundance for the sake of the necessitous. But, it may be asked, why detach ourselves from our wealth? For two reasons, one natural, the other supernatural. The natural reason is that the right to own property is personal, but the use of property is common. God intended the earth to be for the good of all; every human being has a natural and basic right to a portion of earthly goods sufficient to sustain life and to assure him normal and reasonable living conditions. Since this right is more easily and reasonably exercised through private ownership, which dignifies human personality through responsibility, the right to possessions is a natural right, but a secondary one. Translated into concrete terms this means that a man may earn as much wealth as he pleases, but he may not do with it whatever he pleases, simply because every human being has not only a claim in charity but even in justice, to as much of the wealth of the community as is necessary to sustain his life.

The right of a rich man to his wealth is secondary to the right of a starving man to the satisfaction of his human needs. The rich man ought to detach himself from his wealth out of charity for the sake of the poor, and if the need of the poor is acute, the obligation to do so becomes

[7]*Divini Redemptoris.*

one of strict justice. But even charity calls for a sharing of abundance with the needy, for the superfluities of the rich, are the necessities of the poor. As St. Augustine put it: "The burden of the poor is their not having what they absolutely need; the burden of the rich is their having what they do not absolutely need." Scripture records no other reason why Dives lost his soul than because he dined sumptuously each day, was clothed in fine linen, and ignored Lazarus the beggar at his door. He failed to see that the crumbs from his table which were superfluities to him were necessities to Lazarus. In the eyes of the world, Dives must have been a great man, because he was rich; in the eyes of God, Dives was a lost soul, an eternal failure, because he ignored the poor.

The supernatural motive for detachment is that Christians must conform to the example of their Head, Christ. Christ is in the poor. The beggar at the door, the hungry child seeking food, the evicted family, the unemployed street-cleaner, the underpaid and undernourished scrubwoman, the immigrant who speaks poor English -- in each of these the Christian must see the lovely figure of Christ. There is no such thing as case No. 112 in the relief rolls; that case to Christian eyes is Christ. They may not resemble Christ in their virtue, their manners, nor their sanctity, but they do resemble Him in His poverty. By showing our love for their poverty, do we prove that we love Him Who became the poor man of earth. We do not sufficiently realize the transparent character of the poor, and on judgment day, even the just will be surprised to learn that in feeding the hungry, they broke bread with the Master: "I was hungry, and you gave Me to eat; I was thirsty, and you gave Me to drink; I was a stranger, and you took Me in; naked and you covered Me; sick and you visited Me; I was in prison and you came to Me." Even the just in their surprise will ask: "Lord, when did we see Thee hungry and fed Thee; when thirsty and gave Thee to drink? And when did we see Thee a stranger and took Thee in? Or naked and covered Thee? Or when did we see Thee sick or in prison and came to Thee? And the King answering shall say to them: "Amen, I say to you, as long as you did it to one of these my least brethren, you did it to Me." [8]

This Gospel points to a theory and practice of life which is not in harmony with that lived by a great percentage of our population, but which if it were put into practice would revolutionize society in a day. Many rich Christians are good-natured, benevolent, cultivated, and have natural virtues, but few ever give to the poor because they really see Our Lord walking in their worn shoes. We need not be sure the poor are virtuous before we help them, for the demand is that virtue be in us, and if we refuse to give, it is we who are lacking virtue. "Give to everyone that asketh thee." [9] Neither must we consider whether the poor are our enemies or our friends, for Christ is in their poverty and not in their enmity. That is why He said: "And if you do

[8]Matthew 5440
[9]Luke 6:30

good to them that do good to you, what thanks are to you For sinners also do this.... But love ye your enemies: do good and lend hoping for nothing thereby; and your reward shall be great, and you shall be sons of the Highest; for He is kind to the unthankful and to evil." [10]

Even though the gloved hand reaches out for our gift, we nevertheless know we are giving it to the person; in like manner, a dirty hand of the poor man is the glove of the person of Christ. All ye who have, remember! He is walking to your doors on the feet of the hungry; He is asking you for a drink, through the parched tongues of the sick; He is bumping into you at your street corners, in the person of the beggar; He is looking in through your window as a Lazarus, as you dine as a Dives; His mother is knocking at your portals as Mary did at Bethlehem, asking just for an inn where the Saviour might be born. If Bethlehem only knew! If we only suspected! The next time you refuse the poor, ask yourself this question: "What if that man be Christ?"

The Poor:

Now for a word about the poor. Charity is just as binding upon them as on the rich, but in a different way. Charity warns the rich against being selfish, and it warns the poor against being envious. "The poor too, in their turn, while engaged, according to the laws of charity and justice, in acquiring the necessities of life and also in

[10] Luke 6:33. 35

bettering their condition should always remain 'poor in spirit and hold spiritual goods in higher esteem than earthly property and pleasures." [11]

Note that the Church does not say the poor must remain poor; rather she says the poor must better their condition, but at the same time they must remain "poor in spirit." There is a world of difference between the "poor" and the "poor in spirit." The poor are generally the destitute. The "poor in spirit" may be the rich, provided they are detached from their wealth. The Church wants no one to be poor in the sense of miserable -- not even those who take the vow of poverty. That vow does not oblige a priest or a nun to be hungry, nor to be denied a bed and shelter; rather it obliges each to be content with the necessities of life and not to seek more. The poor in spirit who give up everything, by a peculiar paradox possess everything, for there is nothing they desire. No man can have the whole world, but he can renounce the whole world. He cannot possess it, but he can dispossess it; it is not his to own, but it is his to disown; he cannot draw the whole world into his hands, but he can wash his hands of it; there being nothing more he wants, he is, therefore, the richest man in the world. This is the ideal poverty implied by the vow of poverty. But though the Church does not ask everyone to take the vow of poverty, it does want everyone to be "poor in spirit." The poor in our country who would violently dispossess the rich, who join the Communists because they promise to "overthrow

[11] *Divini Redemptoris.*

capitalism by force" and to liquidate all who own, and who sow seeds of hatred against their fellowman, are not the Gospel poor. Their only regret is that they cannot be rich; their souls are just as avaricious as the rich; they are the involuntary poor; the poor who crave to be rich; the enemies of capitalists because they want to be capitalists themselves. They are scandalized at the wealth of others but only after they are tempted by the lust of their possessions. That is why every Communist is at heart a capitalist without any cash in his pockets. He talks more about his hatred of the rich than his love of the poor; more about the evils of the present system than the remedies he has to offer. This group with its hatred of classes is just as much a menace to our civilization as the rich who exploit the poor. The verdict of history is against them; the envious poor who crushed the rich never did anything for the poor man with all their confiscated wealth; they merely transformed individual selfishness into collective selfishness. They, therefore, have no right to condemn the rich; they have never earned the right. No man has a right to condemn the rich until, like our Blessed Lord, he has proven he is free from the passion of wealth.

Charity also enjoins upon the poor a recognition that no human system can ever offer perfect peace and happiness, otherwise earth would be heaven, and this life would not be a novitiate for the next. "Let the poor remember that the world will never be able to rid itself of misery, sorrow, and tribulation, which are the portion of those who seem most prosperous. Patience, therefore is the need of all, that Christian patience which comforts the heart with the divine assurance of eternal happiness." [12]

Lenin ridicules this Christian doctrine by saying that religion asks us "to bear misfortunes uncomplainingly. It thus provides a justification for exploitation as if it were a cheap ticket to Heaven." In other words, it preaches a resignation which is passivity because it teaches those who toil in poverty to be resigned and patient in this world and consoles them with the hope of a reward in heaven."

It simply is not true that religion preaches passivity to unjust conditions. If it did, Leo XIII and Pius XI would never have written their encyclicals in defense of the working man, in which the former states: "It is the duty of the State to promote in the highest degree the interests of the poor... It is the desire of the Church that the poor should rise above poverty and wretchedness and should better their condition *in this life*, and for this, it strives." As a matter of fact, there has never been written a stronger protest against economic injustices.

The resignation which religion preaches is not passive submission to economic injustices, as Communism contends. Resignation means accepting our lot while working to better conditions by an intelligent understanding of the nature of things. A mother, for example, is resigned to the pettiness and helplessness of her new-born babe; a farmer is resigned to the slow maturing of the seed he sows in the springtime, because

[12]Ibid.

both take into account the nature of things. But because the mother is resigned to infancy, or because the farmer is resigned to the seasons, it does not follow that they are passive or inactive, nor that the mother does not nourish her babe, nor the farmer till his crops. As a matter of fact, they both work intelligently to draw out the perfection of the things committed to their care.

So it is with religion. Religion is resigned to the nature of the world and the nature of man. It knows very well that man is prone to evil, that some selfishness will remain under any economic system, and that no paradise can be built here below. But because religion is resigned to these practical limitations, religion does not refuse to better conditions by infusing virtue into the hearts and souls of men, to the end of making a world where the good can live among the bad, where the rich can live without exploiting the poor and the poor can live without being violently destructive of all wealth, and where the majority can live in a state this side of heroism and martyrdom. Communism, however, refuses to accept the nature of things and thinks it can change them by violence and confiscation. But it is just as foolish to think that by a revolution one can alter the nature of man, as it is to believe that you can alter the nature of a baby by putting a bomb under its cradle, blowing it up, and expecting it to come down a full-grown Bolshevik. In fact, it is just as foolish to try to build a perfect Paradise here below by revolution, as it is to try to dynamite triangles into four-sided figures.

There are certain things to which we must be resigned and the nature of man is one. It is simply because Russia has refused to take account of this one fact that it has failed. All its failures are failures incident to human nature. Since it failed to be resigned to that, it must be resigned to failure.

If the term "opium" deserves to be applied to any. thing it certainly is not to religion. What is the effect of opium? Opium is a drug which puts the intellect and will to sleep and allows only the vegetative and animal functions to continue. A man under the influence of that drug cannot think, cannot resolve, but he can breathe and he can digest.

Now what thing in the world so much puts the mind to sleep, and allows only the animal functions to continue as Communism? It drugs the mind by refusing to allow it to reason from the order of the stars to the Creative Hand that made them; it drugs the mind with propaganda, by creating a public opinion which it represents as the only one possible; it drugs the will by defining liberty as believing what the State believes, and doing what the State dictates, thinking what the State thinks, and enforces that identity by terror. It reduces man to an animal by regarding him as an ant whose business it is to pile up more wealth for the State, it deprives his moral actions of a natural basis by declaring he has no other destiny than that of a faithful horse in a collectivist farm. It then upsets that belief by mummifying Lenin, for if the destiny of both Lenin and a horse is the same, why glorify one more than another?

As long then as opium remains what it is, Communism must be called the opium of the people.

By holding up the future state, religion makes man active and not passive as the Marxists contend. As a matter of fact, only those beings who have some idea of the future are active. A machine never contemplates what it will do tomorrow, hence it never lays up an extra supply of oil for the next day's labor. An animal has very imperfectly some sense of the future inasmuch as its instinct makes it search for prey. Man has a definite idea of the future because he has ideals and every ideal transcends time. That is why man's activity is greater than that of the animal. His activity will increase in direct ratio and proportion with his grasp of the future and his determination to achieve a future ideal. A young man of twenty, for example, resolves to become a doctor by thirty. This means that an ideal, which is ten years in the future, makes him active for ten years and willing to put up with sacrifices in order to attain his degree. If, however, his ideal extended no further than the next meal, he would be active only for a few hours.

If then the future is the cause of activity, and if the greater the ideal the greater the activity, then it is false to say, as Communism does, that religion's emphasis on the future makes a man passive. Even the Communists do not believe it themselves, for they draw up Five Year Plans. What are they but five years of hard work to attain a future ideal? Now if men work hard to complete an earthly plan, then why is it illogical to say they will work hard to attain an eternal plan?

Certainly, that man who believes he has a soul to save, will work hard every moment of his life and will think every thought and will do every deed in the light of that ideal. And that is just precisely what Our Lord meant when He said: "What doth it profit a man if he gain the whole world and lose his immortal soul?" It is not the future then which makes man passive; rather it is that which makes him active. Hence give a man no greater glory than having his body mummified in a glass case, and you will make him as passive as a cow unless you goad him with bayonets. And even then he will ask: "Why should the flowers bloom again in the springtime, and I who am their master, be denied a resurrection allowed to them which I crush under my feet?"

In conclusion, let it be recalled that the spirit of charity is offered as a remedy for Communism, and in particular charity to the poor on the part of the rich. Communism has won its adherents because it capitalizes on the misery of the poor and rightfully protests against many of the injustices of the rich. But the remedy it offers is wrong because it would create, as it did in Russia, a new wealthy class by violent confiscation of property, rather than an orderly society by peaceful distribution of wealth through democratic methods of social justice and charity. A true Christian spirit of generosity which will share superfluities with the poor will do much to combat the deceits of the Communist Popular Front; it will not do everything, because if we had a Paradise in America the Communists would still want to worm their way into it as Lucifer wormed his way into Eden.

The spirit of charity will do much not only to weaken the vindictiveness of those who attack the unfulfilled duties of the rich, but it will also do much to make us live in peace and concord with our fellowman. *The Communist solution is to make the poor hate the rich; the Christian solution is to make the rich love the poor.* The reason why the Communists make the poor hate the rich, is to set society in such a state of chaos that they can establish their dictatorship over the proletariat; the reason why Christians want to make the rich love the poor is that all may enjoy the heritages and benefits of civilization, and in order that the poor man, relieved from the worry of a livelihood, might be free enough to save his soul.

The Communists speak only of the proletariat; the Christian speaks of the poor. The proletariat is the worker who can be used to overthrow existing society and set up a Soviet régime, the poor is every man -- he may even be the Communist who hates you. The proletariat is the abstract -- the mass, the collectivity, the mob that can be thrown into hysteria by their "vanguard and leader" as the Communist Party calls itself; the poor is the concrete -- the personal, the unemployed barber, the sick minister without a pulpit, the Jewish father who has just lost his sole supporting son. The proletariat is a class; the poor is every man -- friend and enemy. The proletariat wants not only his own goods but those of his neighbor; the poor wants to have sufficient of his own goods and believes his neighbor should have the same. The Communist wants to help the proletarian to hasten the revolution; the Christian wants to help the poor to help his salvation. The Communist wants to make the proletarian hate his employer as a thief; the Christian wants to make the employer practice a moral virtue and give to every man his due. The Communist feeds the proletariat to make more wealth for the state; the Christian feeds the poor to leave his soul free to think about something else than a sickle and a hammer.

America is broader and bigger than the proletariat class; it has the poor in it who are not workers and who cannot work. Hence it needs something more than Communism; it needs charity. Hatred and selfishness will not save society because they are essentially destructive; only a spirit of charity poured out lavishly from the throne of Christ can so order it that the rich will anticipate the needs of the poor and the poor will be grateful for the rich.

Not to that narrow group called the proletariat have we been sent, but to the poor which includes the proletariat as the animal kingdom includes the horse. The Church recruited her strength from them in the beginning, and it is from them again that she will draw her new strength. As Catholics, we must be conscious of our duty to them as never before, and it is our solemn duty to go down to the masses and build up just as strong and vigorous a body of noble men and women dedicated to peace, their God, and their country, as the Communists would build up a revolutionary proletariat. The banner of lovers of the poor shall not be taken from our hands by those who shriek hatred of the rich. We are born of the Poor Man of Galilee, and lovers of the poor we must be, even though it means the sacrifice of our comfort and the touch of Calvary's cross. Then we need have no fear of the Communists. They are not interested in the poor; they are interested only in wealth. They talk about nothing else; they think about nothing else; they plan on having nothing else, even though they have to steal it. Communism is, therefore, the philosophy of the wealthy -- the studied system of making the envious proletariat rich by pillage. The poor they leave to Christ and to us -- and ours they will be even to the end of time.

Chapter IX

Two Revolutions

Underlying the multitudinous social and economic theories of our day, there are only two possible reforms: one is to reform institutions, the other is to reform man.

One begins by blaming institutions. The ills of humanity are thus always charged to a *thing*. Some blame private property for our inequalities, and hence reform it into collective ownership; others blame parliamentary systems, and reform them into a dictatorship; others blame disorganized labor, and reform it into a mass organization; others blame the gold policy, and reform it into a silver policy. In each and every instance the revolution is against something *outside* of man -- his property, his government, his finances. Never once is man blamed for the world's debacle and never once does the reform touch man.

So insignificant is man in this scheme that today the tendency is to *make man fit institutions*. Instead of the State existing for man, man exists for the State. As clay is molded in the hands of the potter, so man is dehumanized and de-personalized and then poured into a dictatorial pattern and comes out identified either with a nation, or a race, or a class. It matters not if whole nations are deprived of liberty, or if millions starve, or if thousands are purged, as long as a theory or policy of government survive. Instead of making the hat fit the head, the modern tendency is to make the head fit the hat, which is only another way of saying that institutions, political themes, dictatorships, must survive even though it means the destruction of man.

The other reform is just the opposite. It believes that the reformation must begin in man. It agrees that there should be a revolution, but maintains that the revolution should not be against something *outside* man, but something *inside* man, namely, his pride, his egotism, his selfishness, his envy, and his avarice. It places the blame not on institutions, but on humanity, not on things but on persons, not on property but on man. Man is always prone to blame someone else; from earliest childhood when he kicked and banged the door because he bumped his nose, to that other childhood when in a game of golf he cursed the demons of hell and the God of heaven because he missed the cup. Now the ball was not to blame, nor the club, nor the demons of hell, nor the God of heaven; it was the golfer himself who was to blame. The world is like the golfer-always blaming everything except the one thing on whom the blame is to be placed, namely, himself.

But transferring blame is no solution. The fault is in man. Hence, what is the use of transferring the title of property from a few capitalists to a few red commissars if you still leave both greedy and dishonest? Why blame the tools when the ruin is caused by the one who misuses them? Why blame parliament when the actions of parliament are really the actions of the human beings who compose it? In other words, remake man and you remake the world and all its institutions.

That is why in this latter view, it is institutions which must be fitted to man. Instead of forcing man into the artificial pattern of a race-state, the race-state must surrender itself and allow man the exercise of his liberty. Instead of cowing men with bayonets into slavish obedience to a dictatorship over the proletariat, the dictatorship must give up and allow men to be captains and masters once again of their own fate and destiny. Man is the highest creature in creation; he must live regardless of what worldly institution fails; let themes crackle and go up in smoke; let race worship be dissipated like a fog; let enslaving tyrants bombing their way to proletarian thrones be delivered over to everlasting mummification. None of these is as important as man. Let them all fade away as an unsubstantial pageant; what matters is that man survive, for the world and all that is in it is not worth one immortal soul: "For what doth it profit man if he gain the whole world and lose his immortal soul?"

These two contrasting ideologies met in conflict centuries ago in the time perspective of those three days from Good Friday to Easter Sunday. On one side was Our Lord Who came to preach the necessity of remaking man. He placed the blame for chaos not on money but on men; not on politics but on politicians; not on military strategy but on generals; not on dictatorship but on dictators; not on money-lending but on the money-lenders. All these things had to be revolutionized, but the way to revolutionize them is first to revolutionize man. Therefore He said nothing about slavery, but He said everything about the dignity of a man; He said nothing about finances, but everything about the rich men who like Dives luxuriate their way to hell; He said nothing about violence against capitalism, but everything about violence against the selfishness of the man who lays up treasures which rust consumes and moths eat. He said nothing against armament, but He said everything against the man who draws his sword in hate. It was man who had to be reborn, to die to himself, to take up his daily cross, to cut off his hands of selfishness, to pluck out his eyes of envy, to become as a servant if he were a master, to bless if he were persecuted, to forgive if he were reviled, to rejoice if he were hated and above all else to die to his lower life, like a seed falling to the ground that he might live in the newness of a resurrected life where man lives even when the world dies. And so, He left Pilate in his judgment seat, Herod with his court, Annas with his Sanhedrin, soldiers on their streets, Caesar on his throne, and chose twelve men whom He remade in His Image and filled with His Spirit and sent them out to conquer the world and its institutions.

Naturally, the world which placed its hope in the reformation of institutions could hardly tolerate the doctrine of Him Who placed the hope for reformation in a new man. Just as today Germany sacrifices man for its idiotic race worship, and Russia sacrifices man for its anti-human State Capitalism, so too then the world believed that that Man should be sacrificed rather than their institutions perish. That is why, when Our Blessed Lord appeared before the judges, they all agreed that He should die rather than that their institutions should perish. Caiaphas was anticipating Krylenko when he said that it was fitting that Christ should die rather than the national institutions be endangered. The Pharisees, though they hated Caesar with a bitter hate, said it was fitting that Christ should die rather than loyalty to Caesar be impugned. Pilate agreed that He should die rather than his political prestige with Caesar be challenged. Annas and Caiaphas, Herod and Pilate could not agree on which institution should survive; they could only agree that He Who sought to reform man should die. Things must live even though the human perish! It was like the cry of Hitlerism and Stalinism of our day -- Dictatorship must live even though thousands perish.

In perfect keeping with that philosophy of subjecting the human to the institutional, the judges nailed Him to a cross. A man was fitted to a thing; thus a God Incarnate was crucified to a cross; a Divine Life was sacrificed to a policy; a soul went down before Caesar. It was all so very clear -- man must perish, the world must survive. They wanted Him to condemn Caesar or to condemn Israel, but not to blame their sinful souls. They would have welcomed Him had He said the fault was in things; but they crucified Him because He said the fault was in man.

Good Friday then was the world's answer to God the temporary triumph of those who kill man that institutions may live. It was like a sick patient killing the physician because he found the source of the disease. But by a peculiar and beautiful paradox, in crucifying Him, they proved that He was right and they were wrong. They wanted Him to blame Caesar, but not to blame themselves. They would have welcomed Him if He said the fault was in things, but they crucified Him because He said the fault was in man.

Good Friday was the world's answer to God. They lifted Him on the cross because His Goodness was their greatest reproach. The mediocre survive; the good are persecuted. The same thing in an evil man which makes him turn a deaf ear to the warning of conscience makes the world nail Innocence to a tree when it accuses it of sin. He said the way to transform the world was to transform man. They so hated that idea that they killed Him, but in killing Him they transformed Him; by the power of God, they changed mortality into Immortality. The cross was the very thing, He said, a man must carry in order to be re-made. They gave Him the cross and He turned the ignominy of Good Friday into the triumph of Easter Sunday. He said a man must die in order to live; they gave Him death and He lived anew. He said that unless the seed, falling to the ground dies, it remaineth alone; they planted Him as a seed on Friday, and on Easter He rose like the flower breaking the sod at springtime in the newness of Divine Life. He said that no one shall be exalted unless He is humbled; they humbled Him in Calvary and He became exalted over an empty grave. They sowed His body in dishonor and He rose in glory; they sowed it in weakness and it rose in power.

He is the same and yet He is different. He is the same Son of God, the same Son of Mary, the same Jesus Who suffered under Pontius Pilate, was crucified, died, and was buried. And yet He is no longer the same. He is no longer subject to pain, to crucifixion, to death. He is glorified in His Human Nature, fit to sit at the Right Hand of the Father to make intercession for us. One scene, in particular, reveals the Resurrected Man -- the scene is the upper room of Jerusalem where the Apostles are gathered. In the expressive language of Scripture "the doors were shut" -- shut because they feared the military who might have accused them of stealing the body from the grave; shut because fearful of the mobs, for not so long before it was then "the hour of darkness." Suddenly, "Jesus came and stood in the midst of them and said to them: Peace be unto you." Early, when He appeared to the women, He said: "Rejoice" for they were in grief. Now He says "Peace" to the disciples, for they were in fear. By peace He meant the certainty of sin forgiven, the tidings of death overcome, the restoration of communion with the living, the hush of terror and doubt, and above all else the tranquility of order.

"And when He had said this, He showed them His hands, and His feet and side." [1] He was the same Jesus they knew;

[1] John 20:20 Luke 24:36-43.

the same Man Who was crucified, that is why He showed them hands that had busied themselves with His Father's business; hands they had seen placed on the heads of little children; feet that carried Him to mountain tops for all-night vigils of prayer; feet that had hastened to the side of the wretched and stood near the forlorn; feet that had failed Him in Gethsemane under a load of sorrow; a side that was whole as John leaned against it to hear the very secrets of the Heart of God; a side that John a little later saw opened with a lance that Love might stand revealed and that like another open door in another Noah's ark, all men might enter for escape from the flood of sin. He was the same Man, and yet He was different for He now came to them through closed doors. The death marks proved His identity with the cross, but they also proved His power over it, for wounds are now scars to prove that Love is stronger than death. It was no ghost the Apostles were seeing, despite His entrance through closed doors, despite His celestial radiance and the glory of His Resurrection. He had lived the Gospel He had preached: The way to reform the world is to reform man. Within forty years after, the world that put Him to death was dead, but He lives on. And thus there emerges from Easter the lesson: *The world dies, but the Resurrected Man lives on.*

A dozen times in history this lesson has been repeated. First of all, when Peter and Paul went out to preach the Gospel of the Resurrection, the paganism of the Roman Empire answered by persecution. It refused to believe that pagan man needed reformation. In order the better to show its belief in the subjection of man to institutions, it fitted the Christians to Caesar's rack as it had fitted Christ to Caesar's cross. There must have been those who believed that the way to save Christianity was to reform the Roman Empire -- but not the Apostles. They had the mandate from their Master to regenerate man. Instead of preaching revolution against Caesar, they preached revolution against sin. Instead of attacking the indignities of the Roman citizenship, they preached the glories of the citizenship of the saints in the Kingdom of God. Peter and Paul stood by their graves already dug but their Good Friday was changed into Easter Sunday. The paganism of the Roman Empire died and Christianity lived, for *the world dies but the Resurrected Man lives on.*

Then came the Church's conflict with the institution of slavery in which man was a chattel and a piece of merchandise like the grain he sold. Never once did the Church preach a revolution against slave owners; but unceasingly did it preach the inherent dignity of man. St. Paul wrote to a slave owner asking him to take back a slave, but to remember that the slave, now baptized, was a child of God and an heir of heaven. Under the influence of the Church, Constantine and Justinian passed a series of humane laws forbidding the separation of slaves from their families. Later on, the Order of Our Lady of Ransom redeemed half a million slaves in four centuries. In 1537 Paul III declared that the natives of America had equal rights before God with their conquerors. Slowly the

Christian ferment of human personality entered society and in 1610 St. Peter Claver landed at Cartagena in the Caribbean Sea, the chief slave market of the world, where slaves were sold in bundles of sixes. For thirty-eight years St. Peter Claver labored among them, washed them, dressed their wounds, made their beds and mothered them, and preached to them their dignity before God. And that man of God, so full of God, so reformed himself and those about him that there passed away slavery like paganism, for *the world dies but the Resurrected Man lives on.*

To take a final example. The world today is bent solely on reforming institutions; it is making man exist for the State or the race or the class, instead of making the State exist for man. Set up against it, as on the first Good Friday is the Church which, because it upholds the dignity of man and his vocation to a supernatural end, is accused of being counter-revolutionary. That is why the Church is momentarily going down to her death in Mexico, Spain, Germany, and Russia. These nations know they cannot master man until they crush the Church which says that man is also a child of God. But be not discouraged. In less than two decades these institutions will perish; Nazism will be as dead as Bismarck's Kulturkampf; red Madrid will be as dead as the Russian Revolutionists of 1917; red Russia is dying already. The lesson is ever true: *the world dies, but Resurrected Man lives on.*

Choose your revolution. Either revolt against things

or you will revolt against yourself. If you revolt against things and set up new things they will die, for the world always dies as Jerusalem died, as paganism died, as slavery died, and as Communism is dying. If you revolt against yourself on the Good Friday of your mortified life, you will live glorious with the Risen Christ, for only those who are made conformable to His Passion will be made conformable to His Resurrection.

Leave man as he is, and reform institutions and you will have a tremendous following -- you will have in your retinue the race of those who throw away their tools because they clumsily pinched their fingers. You will be called a liberator by men because you still leave them free to be selfish, mean, and base; because you will still allow the robbers to rob, the thieves to steal, and the agitators to agitate. But your following will be the following of death, *for the world and its concupiscence dies, but only the Resurrected Man lives on.*

But if you reform yourself, do violence to yourself and not your neighbor, do violence to your envy and not his home; do violence to your avarice and not his family; do violence to your sin and not his shop, then your regeneration of your lower self will make more glorious the life you seemed to have destroyed for *the world dies, but the Resurrected Man lives on.*

It is man who must live; man made to the Divine Image; man refashioned by the Incarnation; man valued at an infinite price by Redemption; man nourished by Divine Life in the Eucharist. Save man and you save the world! Save him from his de-humanization by economics, from his

De-personalization by atheism; save him from subjection to race, class, and nation; *save man and you save the world!* Keep the Divine Image in him and not even a crucifixion or a sealed tomb can keep him down; keep the Divine in him and he will rise; ignore it and he will be buried beneath the collapse of our institutions.

It is to the saving of man by spiritual regeneration that Easter calls us, that is why true Christianity is the greatest revolution in the world. It is easy to topple thrones; it is easy to burn palaces; it is easy to shout, "Down with classes;" it is easy to destroy civilization; these revolutions only touch the surface of things. But try to topple selfishness; try to overcome your greed; try to destroy sin and if you succeed in burying your lower self in the Calvary of Christian mortification to live the renewed Christ life, you will be one of the greatest revolutionists in the world -- you will be a saint!

Each revolution has its symbol -- the clenched fist or the folded hands. If you want to reform institutions and to forget about your own need of reformation, you will choose the symbol of the clenched fist. The clenched fist -- the symbol of hatred and bitterness; the symbol of the burning tabernacles, the pillaged homes, the desecrated corpses; the symbol of that which tears down and has nothing to put in its place; the one gesture that turns the hand of man so which was meant to be an instrument of art into that which closely resembles the claw of a beast. The other symbol of those who believe in the internal revolution against baseness and the need of regeneration from on high is that of the folded hands. Folded hands cannot strike for they were not made for offense; they cannot protect for they were not made for defense; they can only imprecate; only pray; ten Gothic spires; a carnal decade aspiring heavenward in petition for the souls of men.

And by and through those folded hands may all the race of the clenched fists -- the race of Cain -- come beneath that cross where there is a Man outstretched as a banner of salvation. By and through the charities and prayers of those folded hands, may those clenched fists, as it were, open and release their hate. And then those Hands which were nailed by hate will detach themselves and fold themselves together, not in judgment, but in embrace, that all the world may know how sweet is the love of Christ.

Selected Bibliography on Communism

PERSONALITIES

Karl Marx, Otto Ruhle (George Allen & Unwin, London, 1929). - Interesting life, but partly from the Freudian point of view.

Karl Karl Marx, Boris Nicolaievsky and Otto Maenchen-Helfen (J. P. Lippincott, Philadelphia, 1936). - Communistic.

Karl Marx, Edward H. Carr (J. M. Dent and Sons, London, 1934). - The best work on the life of Marx.

Stalin, Isaac Don Levine (Newnes, London, 1931. Second edition, 1936 Blue Ribbon Books, N. Y., 1931). - Good.

Lenin, William C. White (Harrison Smith and Robert Haas, N. Y., 1936). - Uncritical, but good.

Lenin, Red Dictator, Vernadsky (Yale University Press, 1931). - A documented life.

Lenin, Ralph Fox (Harcourt, Brace & Co., 1934). - Glorifies Lenin

Lenin, Christopher Hollis (Bruce, 1938). - The best book on the subject.

BOOKS HELPFUL FOR CRITICAL APPRECIATION OF COMMUNISM

The Will to Freedom, Ross J. S. Hoffman (Sheed & Ward). - Study of the Liberal State, Fascism and Communism, and Liberty and Authority.

The Christian Social Manifesto, Joseph Husslein, S.J. (Bruce *and Co.).- A good explanation of the Rerum Novarum and Quadragesimo* Anno.

Freedom in the Modern World, Jacques Maritain (Scribners, 1936). - A profound philosophical study of Freedom and Culture which contains basic principles for refuting Communism, particularly on the subject of Freedom.

Bolshevism in Theory and Practice, Waldemar Gurian (*Macmillan Co., 1932).& The Future of Bolshevism, Waldemar Gurian (Sheed & Ward,* 1936). - Both extremely valuable. The latter discusses Nazism and Fascism in relation to Communism.

The End of Our Time, Nicholas Berdyaev (Sheed & Ward, 1933). - Thesis: We are now living at the end of the Renaissance.

The Fate of Man in the Modern World, Nicholas Berdyaev (Sheed & Ward, 1936). - A study of how Communism collectivizes and dehumanizes *man*.

The Great Encyclicals of Leo XIII (Benziger, 1905).   The Truth and Error of Communism, H. G. Wood (Student Christian Movement Press, London). - A fairly good popular presentation of Marxian principles and refutation.

Medical Socialism, Bede Jarrett (Burns, Oates & Washbourne, London, 1935). - A Catholic study of the medieval notion of property and the *medieval "Communists."*

Freedom versus Organization, Bertrand Russell (W. W Norton, N. Y., 1934). - Chapters 17-20 give a criticism of Marxism. The author is not otherwise sound.

Science of Ethics, Michael Cronin (Benziger, 1917). - Criticism of Socialism and Communism, Vol. 2, pp. 113-297.

The Servile State, Hilaire Belloc (Constable and Co., London, 3rd Edition, 1927). - Still one of the best works on the consequences of Capitalism.

A Survey of Socialism, F. J. C. Hearnshaw (Macmillan Co.,1929). - Good history of Socialism and Marxism and their defects. Also contains an excellent bibliography.

An Essay on the Restoration of Property, Hilaire Belloc (Sheed & *Ward, 1936). - Indispensable.*

*Re-organization of Social Economy, Nell-Bruening (Bruce,*1936). - By all odds the best commentary yet published on the Papal Encyclicals treating the social questions of the day. Im*portant.*

Christian Social Reconstruction, Dom Virgil Michel, O.S.B. (Bruce Publishing Co., N. Y., 1936). - A popular analysis and epitome of the principle of Quadragesimo Anno.

The Church and Labor, John A. Ryan and Joseph Husslein, S.J. (Macmillan Co., 1924). - Pontifical and Episcopal letters bearing on the subjects of Church and Labor supplemented by an interpretation by the editors.

The State and The Church, John A. Ryan and Moorhouse F. X. Millar, S.J. (Macmillan Co., 1936). - Collection of essays on the State, Liberty, Democracy, Americanism, and International Relations.

Democratic Industry, Joseph Husslein, S.J. (P. J. Kenedy & *Sons, 1919). -* A practical study of social history.

Investigation of Nazi Propaganda Activities and Other Propaganda Activities, House of Representatives Report 153, Seventy-Third Congress. Union Calendar No. 44.

Also, *Report 2290 of Seventy-First Congress*. Extract on Communist Activities distributed by R.O.T.C. Association of the U.S., Lt. Col. Orvel Johnson, Woodward Building, Washington, D. C.

The Good Society, Walter Lippmann, pp. 45-91 (Little, Brown & Co., 1937). - Contains an excellent criticism of collectivism and the totalitarian régime.

Religion and the Modern State, Christopher Dawson (Sheed and Ward, 1933). - Communism, Nazism, and Fascism examined from a Christian point of view. Excellent.

The Catholic Tradition of the Law of Nations, John Eppstein (Catholic Assn. for International Peace, N.C.W.C., Washington, D.C.). - A documentary presentation of the Catholic ideas on Peace, War, and Society of Nations.

The Catholic Social Movement, Henry Somerville (Burns, Oates and Washbourne, 1933). - A presentation of the Catholic Social Movement in Germany, Holland, Austria, France, and Belgium.

Militant Atheism, Most Rev. M. d'Herbigny (S.P.C.K., Northumberland Ave., London, W.C. 2, 1934). - A presentation of atheistic propaganda in India, Peru, Canada, Bulgaria, Germany, and Belgium.

We or They, Hamilton Fish Armstrong (Macmillan Co., 1936). - Thesis: Conflict of the present day is between Democracy and Dictatorship. Strong criticism of Fascism and Communism.

Moscow over Methodism, Rembert G. Smith, D.D. (Published by Author, Afton, Oklahoma). - An attack on Communism by a Methodist who reveals influ*ence of Communism on Methodism.*

Dictators and Democracies, Calvin B. Hoover (Macmillan Co., 1937, 110 PP.). - A good criticism of Communism, Fascism, and the Totalitarian *State, by the author of Economic Life in Russia.*

The Crisis of Civilization, Hilaire Belloc (Fordham Press, 1937, 245 PP.). - Defends brilliantly the thesis that the Church is the heart of European civilization. Contains also splendid criticism of Capitalism and Communism and the Catholic solution of distribution. Indispensable.

Tradition and Modernism in Politics, A. J. Penty (Sheed and Ward, N. Y., 1937, 182 PP.). - A series of essays. Three particularly good chapters on Socialism, Communism, and Fascism.

Thunder over Europe, H. Gigon, Ph.D. (Sands and Co., London, 124 pp.). - An elementary but excellent study of Democracy, Bolshevism, Fascism, and Nazism.

The Red Network, Elizabeth Dilling, 53 West Jackson Blvd., Chicago, 1936, 338 pp. - A "Who's Who" and Handbook of Radicalism. Lists all Communist-inspired organizations and biography of leading Communists or Communist sympathizers. Contains a few inaccuracies.

Report on Communist Propaganda in America. Submitted to the United States Government by William Green, President of A. F. of L., Jan. 1935. - Excellent.

Socialism, Ludwig von Mises (Jonathan Cape, London, 1936). - A classic on the subject of an economic and sociological analysis of Socialism.

Unto Cassar, F. A. Voigt (Constable & Co., London, 1938). - A good critical presentation of the subjection of man to the *State under Stalin and Hitler.*

The Proletariat, Goetz A. Briefs (McGraw-Hill Book Co., N. Y., 1938). - A profound study of the origin of the proletariat, the proletariat movement, and its relation to Capitalism.

Creative Revolution, J. F. T. Prince (Bruce & Co., 1937). - A moving plea for a creative revolution founded on the charity of Christ.

The War Against God, Sidney Dark and R. S. Essex (Abingdon *Press, N. Y.).* - A good book on the anti-God movement in the modern world.

Communism and Man, Frank Sheed (Sheed & Ward, N. Y., 1938). - The most solid and yet popular refutation of Communism that has been done in English. Concerned principally with the Communist distortion of human nature.

God, Man and the Universe, Kologriwof, S. J. and Ambruzzi, S. J. (Geo. E. J. Coldwell, Ltd., London, 1937). - A chapter for chapter answer to a Soviet work on Atheism. *Very good.*

The Metaphysical Foundations of Dialectical Materialism, Charles J. McFadden, Ph.D., O.S.A. (Catholic University of America, Washington, D. C. 1938). - A sound Scholastic refutation of Marxist philosophy.

The Problem of Solidarism in St. Thomas, Sister Mary Joan of Are Wolfe, Ph.D. (Catholic University of America, 1938). - A solid critical appreciation of Individualism and Collectivism in the light of St. Thomas.

HISTORICAL BACKGROUND

The Rise of Liberalism, Harold J. Laski (George Allen & Unwin, London). Also published in America, 1936. - A critical presentation of Liberalism from the "left" point of view. Very good.

Liberalism, L. T. Hobhouse (Henry Holt & Co. Home University Library, No. 16). - Less historical than Laski and more partial to Liberalism.

Catholicism, Protestantism and Capitalism, A. Fanfani (Sheed &Ward, 1935). - Splendid Catholic work on the difference between the social policies of Catholicism, Protestantism, and Capitalism.

The Protestant Ethic in the Spirit of Capitalism, Max Weber (Allen & Unwin, London, 1930). - A study of the influence of Calvinism on Capitalism.

Religion and the Rise of Capitalism, R. H. Tawney (John Murray, London, 1925). - Shows effect of Protestantism on the modern world. A classic on the subject.

The Russian Church, J. N. Danzas (Sheed & Ward, 1936). - A history of the Russian Church up to the time of the Revolution.

The Fall of the Russian Empire, Edmund A. Walsh, S.J. (Little, Brown & Co., Boston). - An authoritative work by the former head of the Papal Commission to Russia.

Documents of Russian History, 1914-1917, Frank Alfred Golder (D. Appleton Century Co., N. Y., 1922).

Equality, R. H. Tawney (Allen & Unwin, London, 1931). Thesis: The French Revolution solved the problem of political inequality but not the problem of economic inequality.

The Origin of Russian Communism, Nicholas Berdyaev (Geoffrey Bles: Centenary Press, London, 1937). - An analysis of Russian thought of the 19th century and the differences between Marxian Communism and Russian Communism.

The History of the Russian Revolution, Leon Trotsky (Simon and Schuster, 1936, 3 volumes in 1). - A rather uninspired account of the Russian Revolution.

FACTS ON RUSSIA

Russia's Iron Age, William H. Chamberlin (Little, Brown & Co., 1935). - One of the finest arsenals of facts against Communism, by one who lived in Russia for twelve years.

The Russian Revolution, W. H. Chamberlin, 2 vols. (Macmillan Co., 1935). - Well documented and authoritative. Important

Soviet Russia, William H. Chamberlin (Little, Brown & Co., Boston, 1931, Revised Edition, 1935). - A good presentation of the immediate background of the Revolution and life under the Soviets.

Our Country, Our People, and Theirs, M. E. Tracy (Macmillan, 1938). - The finest work in English on the subject of the superiority of the American system over Nazism, Fascism, Communism. Indispensable.

Prisoner of the O.G.P.U., George Kitchin (Longmans, Green & Co., 1935). - The personal experiences of terror and torture in the O.G.P.U. prison camps during the years 1928–1932.

Communism, Harold J. Laski (Henry Holt & Co., New York, 1927). - A clear presentation of Communist with some profound criticisms.

Under the Bolshevik Uniform, Vladimir Lozarevski (Thornton Butterworth, Ltd., London, 1936). - Factual study of Russia by a former Russian soldier. Good.

Human Life in Russia, Ewald Ammende (George Allen & Unwin, Ltd., 1936, London). - A documented history of famine in Russia.

Russia under the Red Flag, G. M. Godden (Burns, Oates & Washbourne, Ltd., London, 1929). - A strong indictment of Communism's attitude toward Religion, Liberty, Industry, and Land.

The Communist Attack on Great Britain, G. M. Godden (Burns, Oates & Washbourne, Ltd., London, 1935).

Contemporary Russia, 92 Fleet St., London, E.C. 4 (Quarterly $1.25 per year). - An excellent factual and documented account of economics and politics in the Soviet Union.

I Visit the Soviets, E. M. Delafield (Harpers, 1937). - A gossipy, undocumented but critical story of a woman's visit to Soviet Russia.

The Whited Sepulchre, Carlo von Kügelgen (Butterworth Press, London, 1935). - An account of the trials of an evangelical minister in Russia.

The Calvary on Golgotha (Published for the Commission Pro Deo by Margaret Watson, Ltd., 15 Palace Chambers, Bridge St., Westminster, S.W. I). - Pamphlet on the life and suffering of the Russian clergy today.

Communism in Germany, Adolf Ehrt, 1933. - A government publication of Communist activities on the eve of the Nazi Revolution. Documented.

Collectivism, A False Utopia, William H. Chamberlin (Macmillan, 1937). - The story of how Liberty and Democracy have been trampled underfoot by Fascism, Nazism, and Communism. Particular reference is made to Communism. Factual. One of the best books on the subject.

I Speak for the Silent, Vladimir Tchernavin (Hale, Cushman & Flint, N. Y.). - An absorbing story of a former Russian intellectual in a labor camp.

Escape from the Soviets, Tatiana Tchernavin (E. P. Dutton & Co., N. Y.). - The writer is the wife of the above-mentioned author. Most interesting first-hand story of Russian prisons and the fear of the Russian people.

Russia in Chains, Ivan Solonevich (Williams & Norgate, London, 1938, 312 pp.). - An absorbing story by an escaped Soviet who spent eight years in a concentration camp. Estimates at five million the number of Russians presently imprisoned in camps.

W. Soviet Women, Tatiana Tchernavin (E. P. Dutton & Co., N. Y., 1936). - Portraits of various women under Communism.

I Was a Soviet Worker, Andrew Smith (E. P. Dutton). - A former member of the American Communist Party tells how he actually found Russia after going there to live. A work which should have enormous appeal to the working man. Very readable.

The Bolshevik Revolution, Bunyan & Fisher (1934). - A rich source of documentation on the 1917-1918 Revolution. Absolutely reliable. Important.

Intervention, Civil War and Communism in Russia, James Bunyan (Johns Hopkins University Press, 1936). - Another documented work of the highest technical order, covering the period on subjects indicated between April and December 1918.

The Tragedy of Russia, Will Durant (Simon and Schuster, N. Y., 1933). - Critical impression of Russia, written after a visit.

Russia, Hans Von Eckhardt (Knopf, N. Y., 1932).- Objective, comprehensive historical work.

The Last Stand, Edmund Walsh, S.J. (Little, Brown & Co., Boston) - Explanation of the theory of the Soviet State and its practical application.

The Bolshevik Persecution of Christianity, Francis McCullagh (John Murray, London, 1924). - A first-hand account of religious trials.

Soviet Man-Nowo, Helen Iswolsky (Sheed & Ward, 1936). - A very good study of the recent changes of attitudes in Russia.

Russia, U.S.S.R. and Soviet Union Today, Malevsky-Malevitch (Paisley Press, N. Y.). - An authoritative array of economic and political facts about Russia, with criticism. Important. Technical. No other book gives such authoritative statistical information concerning U.S.S.R.

Official Report on Atrocities in Southern Spain, July, and August 1936 (Published by Committee of Investigations appointed by National Government at Burgos, 4th Edition, Eyre and Spottiswoode, London, 1936).

Criminal Syndicalism, Student Americaneers (P. O. Box 456, Columbus, Ohio). - A Catechism of Communism in sixty-three pages, compiled from a Communist Manual. Shows the destructive and subversive character of Communism.

The World Problem (Published by the Vatican Press). Formerly called Letters of Rome. - A monthly journal describing Communist activities. Can be subscribed for through Rev. Charles Leahy, Loyola High School, 1901 Venice Blvd., Los Angeles, Calif. $1.50 per year.

Assignment in Utopia, Eugene Lyons (Harcourt, Brace & Co., N. Y., 1937, 648 pp.). - Former Communist propagandist and chief of the United Press Correspondents in Russia tells the story of how his belief in Communism was shattered by the impact with the Soviet World. A magnificent work.

The Failure of Socialism in Russia, Max Eastman (Little, Brown & Co., Boston, 1936). - A strong factual and documented account of the failure of Communism in Russia written by a Trotskyite.

Russia Twenty Years After, Victor Serge (Hillman Curl, N. Y., 1937, 298 pp.). - A former member of the Executive Committee of the Communist International who is now a follower of Trotsky reveals factually the failure of Communism in Russia.

I Search for Truth in Russia, Sir Walter Citrine (George Routledge & Sons, London, 1936, 360 pp.). - An indispensable objective treatment of living conditions, wages, hours, etc., in Russia, by the General Secretary of the Trade Union Congress.

Return from U.S.S.R., André Gide. (Alfred A. Knopf, 1937, 94 PP.). - A former Communist sympathizer after a visit to Europe confesses: "I doubt whether in any country in the world, even Hitler's Germany, thought be less free, more bowed down, more terrorized, more vassalized."

The Revolution Betrayed, Leon Trotsky (Doubleday, Doran & Co., N.Y., 1937, 308 PP.). - A factual study by Lenin's general of the failure of Communism in Russia.

Proletarian Journey, Fred E. Beal (Hillman Curl, Inc., 1937, 352 pp.). - A personal account of an ex-Communist, convinced by Russian and American experiences that Communism is a failure.

Communism and Anti-Religion, J. de Bivort de la Saudée (Burns, Oates and Washbourne, London, 1938). - A documented proof that Communism is atheistic and anti-religious. One of the best works on the subject.

Labor under the "Ism" (Published by Transportation Association of America, 400 West Madison Street, Chicago, 1937, 48 PP.). - A comparative study shows how much better labor is under democracy rather than under Fascism, Nazism, or Communism.

The American League against War and Fascism, Hillman M. Bishop (527 West 110 Street, New York City, 51 pp.). - A study in Communist tactics showing the above League, which has since changed its name to "The League For Peace and Democracy," is a Communist-front organization.

Isms (Published by American Legion, Indianapolis, Indiana). A documented account of subversive activities in the United States.

Catholicism, Communism and Dictatorship, C. J. Eustace (Benziger Bros., 1938). - A short study of totalitarian systems in relation to the Church.

Soviet Tempo, Violet Connally (Sheed & Ward, N. Y., 1938). - A first-hand report of conditions in Russia by a visitor.

Tradition and Progress, Ross J. Hoffman (Bruce Publishing Co., 1938). - A series of essays including essays on Property, Totalitarian State, Marxism, and Liberty. Very good.

The Government of the Soviet Union, Samuel N. Harper (Van Nostrand, N. Y., 1938). - A good account of the political structure of Russia.

Report of the Commonwealth of Massachusetts. May 27, 1938 (Legislative Printers, Boston), House Document No. 2100. - A 600-page report of Communist activities in Massachusetts.

Soviet Trade and Distribution, Leonard E. Hubbard. (Macmillan Co., 1938). - An objective, documented study of Soviet organization and the mechanism of distribution.

COMMUNIST PERIODICALS

The Daily Worker, the official Communist daily for the United States (50 East 13th Street, New York City). - International Press Correspondence, published in London but can be procured through the Workers Library. This weekly contains news of the activities of the International Communist Party throughout the world. Indispensable.

The Communist International (Monthly), the official organ of the Executive Committee of the Communist International. Can be obtained from the Workers Library, Publishers.

COMMUNIST LITERATURE

Program of the Communist International 1936 (Workers Library, 50 East 13th Street, New York City). - An invaluable source of information concerning Communism as it really is. Absolutely indispensable.

The Working Class Against Fascism, G. Dimitrov (Workers Library). - The story of how Communism prepared in 1935 to present its revolutionary philosophy in a non-revolutionary way.

The Work of the Seventh Congress, D. Z. Manuilsky (Workers Library). - The story of the new tactics of Communism, viz., present only as much of Communism as any country can presently absorb.

The Youth Movement, O. Kuusinen (Workers Library). "Those whom the gods would destroy they must first make blind," p. 30. Communist Election Platform (Workers Library). - These are the new tactics in action. Notice how this platform differs from the program. Communism has changed the approach, but not its principle.

What is Communism? Earl Browder (Workers Library). & The People's Front, Earl Browder (Workers Library). - Two samples of the new tactics of Communism, talking democracy but meaning dictatorship over the proletariat.

The following are the more important sourcebooks on Marxism and Communism. Issued by the Workers Library, New York:

Capital, 3 vols., Karl Marx.

Civil War in France, Karl Marx.

Communist Manifesto, Karl Marx.

Anti-Duehring, Frederick Engels.

Ludwig Feuerbach, Frederick Engels.

Collected Works, 8 vols., V. I. Lenin.

Foundations of Leninism, Joseph Stalin.

Leninism, 2 vols., Joseph Stalin.

PAMPHLETS

Why Catholics Condemn Communism, Pope Pius XI (National Catholic Welfare Conference, Washington, D.C.).

Communism and Communism and Religion, Rev. Lewis Watt, S.J. (Catholic Truth Society, London).

It Is Happening Here, Most Rev. J. F. Noll, D.D. (Our Sunday Visitor, Huntington, Indiana).

Godless Communism, Rev. J. Roger Lyons, S.J. (The Queen's Work, St. Louis, Mo.).

The Communist Philosophy of Life, Very Rev. A. H. Ryan, D.D. (Browne & Nolan Ltd., Dublin).

Facts about Communism, Edward Lodge Curran, Ph.D. (International Catholic Truth Society, Brooklyn, N. Y.).

I Was A Communist, Alexei B. Liberov, Internaternational Catholic Truth Society, Brooklyn, N. Y.).

Communism in the U. S. A., Rev. Joseph F. Thorning (America Press, N. Y.).

Communism and the Catholic Answer, Rev. John LaFarge, S.J. (America Press, N. Y.).

Communism and American Youth, Harry S. McDevitt (America Press, N. Y.).

Communist Action vs. Catholic Action, H. M. Toole (America Press, N. Y.).

A Catechism of Communism, A Passionist Father (Paulist Press, N. Y.).

Communism and Morals (formerly entitled Morals and Moscow).

Fascism, communism, The U. S. A.

Just What is Communism?

Communism and Union Labor, Rev. Raymond T. Feeley, S.J. (Paulist Press, N. Y.).

The Tactics of Communism.

Communism Answers Questions of a Communist.

Communism and Religion.

Liberty Under Communism, Rt. Rev. Msgr. Fulton J. Sheen (Paulist Press, N. Y.).

Communism -- The Opiums of the People, Rt. Rev. Msgr. Fulton J. Sheen (St. Anthony's Guild Press, Paterson, N. J.).

What's Wrong with the Sit-down Strike? Joseph H. Fichter, S.J. (Paulist Press, N. Y.).

I Saw the Soviet, Frederic Siedenburg, S.J. (Queen's Work, St. Louis, Mo.).

Atheistic Communism (Divini Redemptoris), Pius XI (N.C. W.C., 1312 Mass. Ave., N. W., Washington, D.C.).

Twenty Years of Bolshevism, A correspondent of London Times (Carnegie Endowment, 335-405 West 117th Street, New York).

Present Conditions in Russia, Harold Denney of New York. Communism in the United States, A survey by the N.C.W.C., Washington, D.C.

Communism Unmasked, Amos A. Fries (Published by Author, 3305 Woodley Road, N. W., Washington, D.C.).